EDUCATING SOMALI CHILDREN IN BRITAIN

EDUCATING SOMALI CHILDREN IN BRITAIN

Mohamed H. Kahin

Trentham Books

First published in 1997 by Trentham Books Limited

Trentham Books Limited
Westview House
734 London Road
Oakhill
Stoke on Trent
Staffordshire
England ST4 5NP

© Mohamed H. Kahin

British Cataloguing in Publication Data
A catalogue record for this book is available from the British Library
ISBN: 1 85856 089 6

Designed and typeset by Trentham Print Design Ltd., Chester
and printed in Great Britain by The Cromwell Press Ltd., Wiltshire.

Setting the Scene

The country that used to be known as the 'Somali Democratic Republic' no longer exists. The recent political upheaval and subsequent civil war have resulted in the country's disintegration. The former Northern Region broke away and formed the 'Republic of Somaliland'. The rest of the country, though divided into 'mini-fiefdoms' is now referred to as 'Somalia'. Unless otherwise stated, the term 'Somalia' is used in its broader sense throughout this book.

Dedication

This book is offered with affection as a tribute
to Somali children
who are doing their best in difficult circumstances

Contents

Acknowledgements

The study and research work on which this book is based could not have been undertaken without the generous help of many people and I thank these good friends and colleagues. While it is not possible to acknowledge everyone, a special word of gratitude must go Zuhur Elmi for her encouragement and support which made the book grow out of all proportion to my original idea of a small pamphlet. Additional thanks to Miss Elmi and Amina H. Hassan for their research and contribution on the chapter on Somali Girls at Schools and Circumcision.

Special thanks are also due to Peter Tredwin and Margaret Chan of Hounslow Language Team and Martin Orwin of School of Oriental and African Studies (SOAS) for their valuable comments as I shaped this book and to Jill Rutter of the Refugee Council for her advice. To Gillian Klein, my editor, a special word of gratitude for her encouragement and guidance with shrewd and practical comments.

Lastly, but no means least, special thanks go to the Somali parents and children who directly or indirectly contributed to the writing of the book and whose experience, concerns and comments are incorporated into the book.

Preface

Many of the thousands of Somali refugee children at schools in Britain are beginners in the English language and new to the British education system. Some may be literate in Somali and/or Arabic but many more are semi- or non-literate and have little or no previous schooling. Nearly all receive specialist support of some kind. Their needs seem not unlike those of other bilingual children of similar background but a host of underlying factors appear to undermine the efficacy of any special provision for them.

This book is the result of a broad study and research that stretches back to the early 1990s. It attempts to highlight some of the major constraints and their implications for the education of Somali children and focuses on their needs and concerns.

The first two chapters provide comprehensive background information about Somalia – the geography, history and politics, particularly the educational and socio-cultural aspects of the country.

Chapter 3 looks at the Somali community in Britain and some of the problems it faces. Chapter 4 focuses on language: the Somali language and its oral literature and literacy, and the major problem areas in English for Somali speakers.

Chapter 5 offers a detailed problem analysis and makes recommendations that may begin realistically to address the educational needs of Somali children.

Chapter 6 is devoted to Somali girls and their special needs and concerns, and advises on some of the implications of female genital mutilation. Chapter 7 focuses on selected cases which provide further insights and some moving autobiographical accounts by Somali children.

A comprehensive and up to date directory of Somali organisations in Greater London is included; also a glossary of terms used in the book.

Despite a general awareness concerning the issue of the education for Somali children, there has been a notable lack of practical books on the subject to highlight areas of concern and suggest ways forward. This book has been written in the hope that it will enhance the educational experience of Somali children in Britain.

The book is intended for teachers, both language specialists and mainstream, and for LEAs and other organisations responsible for the education and welfare of Somali children. At the same time, effort has been made to ensure that the information provided is open-ended, to allow readers to pursue the topics in the book in greater depth.

The book will be useful:

In classrooms:

- as a source of personal evidence of the experience of Somali children

- as a resource for curriculum support materials

- as a practical focus for discussion of issues of personal, social and political relevance.

In staff training:

- as a stimulus for discussion in staff training sessions in relation to the special needs of Somali children

- to provide insight and help with understanding the cultural/ linguistic background, family situation, social concerns, etc. of Somali children

In school management:

- as a guide to assess current practices in relation to the needs and concerns of Somali children

- as a source of ideas for helping Somali children to settle in and achieve educational success.

Chapter 1

Somalia: a profile

GEOGRAPHY

Area and Location
Somalia is situated in the north-eastern part of Africa, commonly known as the Horn of Africa. An area of 637,700 sq. km., it shares borders with the Republic of Djibouti in the north-west, Kenya in the south, Ethiopia in the west and the Indian Ocean in the east. The coastline (the second longest after South Africa) stretches about 2,880 km along the Gulf of Aden and the Indian Ocean.

Land
A barren coastal land rises from the Gulf of Aden in the north and southwards along the Indian Ocean littoral. Known as *Guban* – Burnt Land – the northern plains are extremely hot and arid, with sparse vegetation and humid climate. The coastal plains then rise to the great plateau which stretches to the northern and western highlands. This escarpment of highlands, known as the Golis range, dominates the whole physical structure of the Northern regions, now the self-proclaimed Somaliland (see chapter 2). Shimbir Biris, Somalia's highest mountain, in the Surad range of the Sanag region rises to 8,000 feet. Inland, the plateau slopes gently down to the Haud plains. This imposing landscape forms a vast waterless savannah which provides rich pasturage during the rainy season. Further south, there is a flat arid plain, with more fertile land along the riverine areas of Juba and Shabelle, Somalia's only permanent rivers. The Webi Juba enters the Indian Ocean close to Kismayo, just off the Equator; while Webi Shabelle runs parallel to the coast for more than 150 miles before it empties its water in the sand dunes and marshes east of the Juba estuary. Both rivers originate in the Ethiopian highlands.

MAP Somalia – showing the new territorial boundaries

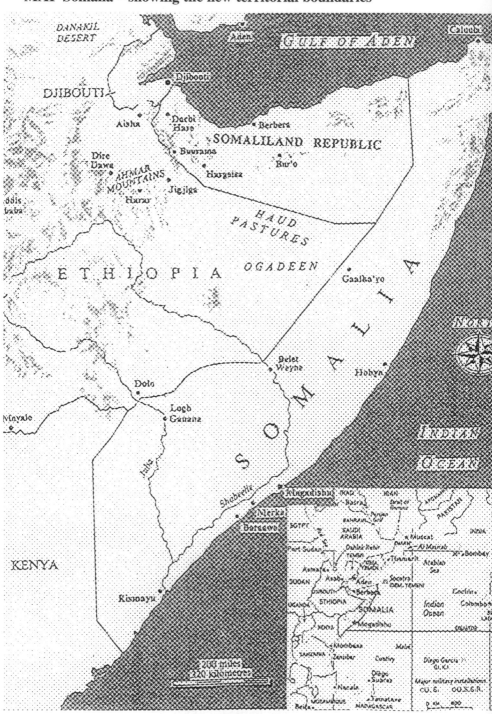

Most of the land in Somalia is suitable only for grazing livestock but in the south the land between the two rivers is the most fertile and well-irrigated. Here most of the staple foodstuffs of the country are grown – corn, millet, rice sugar-cane, citrus fruits, bananas.

Climate

Somalia has a generally semi-arid and tropical climate, with slight seasonal changes in temperature. The average annual temperature is 27°C. It is hotter in the interior and on the Gulf of Aden, but cooler along the Indian Ocean coast. Rainfall is very low, with an average annual rainfall of less than 17 in. The year is divided into four distinct seasons: two wet and two dry. These are determined by the north-east and south-east monsoon winds and the transitional lulls between them. *Gu** (May-June) brings the country's heaviest rains. There are hot and humid periods between monsoons. Rainfall and temperature vary from region to region and from season to season. Rainfall is relatively greater in the northern highlands which also has temperatures below freezing in winter. It is very hot – over 45°C – in the northern coastal plains. Severe droughts are not uncommon and sometimes take a heavy toll of life, like the one in 1974.

Plant and animal life

Somalia has a wide variety of flora and fauna. Acacia trees, mimosa and aloe are common on the Ogo and Haud plains. In the north highlands are small groves of cedar, juniper, wild fig and gob. In the Surad mountains are baobab and the aromatic bushes from which myrrh, frankincense and the sap of euphoria are derived, thus giving the country its historical reference as the land of spices – 'Punt Land'. In the riverine areas in the south, equatorial plants grow such as mangrove, fig trees, kapola and papaya. Palm, coconut, pine and juniper are common features in most of the urban landscape.

The fauna of Somalia include large animals such as elephant, lion, giraffe, leopard, rhinoceros and hippopotamus and game animals such as deer, gazelles, dik-dik, kudu and oryx. Somalia also has rich birdlife, regarded by ornithologists (e.g. Schels, 1992) as the most beautiful in Africa. The most common birds are the ostrich, guinea fowl, bustard, partridge and green pigeon. Kites, crows, ravens and pigeons are

* for explanation of abbreviations and terms in italics, see GLOSSARY

common in most urban centres. Heron, white egret, kingfisher and storks are found in the riverine forest and sparrow weavers, shrikes and bee-eaters in the savannah rangeland. Birds of prey found throughout Somalia include eagles, kites, vultures, owls and hawks.

Somalia, with its long coastline and large continental shelf has an abundant marine life including rockfish, tuna, red snapper and mackerel, lobster, crab and shrimps, sharks and whales.

FACT FILE

*   **Location**: In the north-eastern coast of Africa.

*   **Area**: 637,700 sq. km.

*   **Climate**: Generally arid and tropical; irregular rainfall; hot between monsoons; frequent droughts.

THE PEOPLE

Ethnically, in terms of linguistic and cultural affiliation, Somalis belong to Hamitic stock. Their closest kinsfolk are the surrounding people in Ethiopia and Eriteria – the Afar and the Oromo (Lewis, 1993). Typically, Somalis are tall and slender with fine facial features and skin colour varying from jet black to light brown. Somalis are regarded as independent, tactful and noble in bearing. Population data and vital statistics are generally imprecise and incomplete. The last census (in fact, the only one ever taken!) in 1975 was not reported and its count of the rural population was based on sample enumeration. Somalia's 1994 estimated population was 8,050,000. The country is sparsely, and unevenly, populated. The North-west and the southern coastal belt and riverine areas are the most densely populated.

The Somalis are primarily a pastoral nomadic people who strive to make a living in a hot climate and an unforgiving terrain, much of it desert. Three-fifths of the population lead nomadic or semi-nomadic lives, while many of the remainder who cultivate, particularly in the fertile riverine areas, also keep livestock. Because of the intense competition for scarce resources, they are extremely individualistic, scornful of danger and hunger, and they are constantly engaged in blood feuds or war with neighbouring people (Lewis, 1984). Despite the nomadic mode of life, Somali sub-clans are traditionally associated with a given territory. However, such territory, often defined by the cycle of nomadic migration, is arbitrary in demarcation, resulting in occasional conflict over water and pasturage.

Then there are the townspeople and agriculturists of the urban centres, especially along the coast, where intense and prolonged intimacy with the Islamic tradition has rendered the culture highly organised and religiously orthodox. Urbanisation is, however, limited both in scope and extent and the nomadic tradition still predominates. Moreover, there is a very important form of kin network between the rural and urban areas. As migration to urban areas has increased, contacts have been kept up and it is not uncommon for relatives or kin groups to draw on one another when they need help.

The Somalis are a highly homogenous people, united by language, culture and religion as well as common descent. In terms of ethnic affiliation, the Somalis generally stand out as distinctive and find themselves in limbo. The geographical location of their country on the African continent seems to have little relevance to their cultural inclination to Arabia. This, however, appears an over-simplification of complex issues of culture and identity and embraces the prevalent social and racial attitudes of the interacting parties. In an African setting, a Somali may feel somewhat out of place; within an Arab setting, although sharing a great deal, they equally experience estrangement. The historical and socio-cultural background of the Somali people is therefore a complex phenomenon and in many respects unique. Outside Somalia, the dynamics of the situation would, however, dictate attitudinal change and an identification or alliance with one or other party. Whatever the case, this would definitely have implications for the education of Somali children, underpinning issues of identity and social integration.

Despite the apparent unity, deep division along tribal lines splits Somali society. First is the clan family, which sub-divides into a clan, sub-clan and finally into extended families.

The main clans comprise:

- The Isaq, who live in the north

- The Dir, in the north-west

- The Darod, in the north-east and south-west

- The Hawiye, on the east central coast

- The Digil and Rahanwein on the south hinterland.

All these Somali clans are notionally united in a single genealogy through which they trace a common ancestry. In Somali society, the clan system is undoubtedly very important and forms the basis of the traditional social and political structure in which power was generally decentralised and rested with the elders (Lewis, 1994; Cassallini, 1982). Clan family stresses corporate rights and obligations and provides members with mutual support during feuds or conflict. It also serves as a social support system, though its practical benefits are often limited within the confines of close kin. Relationships among clan and sub-clans is based on the principle of contracts (*xeer*), enshrined in the Somali customary law.

Lineage segmentation has the potential for both integrative and divisive mechanisms which underpin the fluid and shifting allegiance characteristic of Somali politics and social life (cf. Samater, 1991). Because of the wide geographical dispersion of the clan family, it is usually the *reer* (sub-clan) that provides the most meaningful social and political structure. A natural spin-off from this sub-clan entity are the inter-lineage alliances, known as the *dia*-paying group. *Dia* or *mag* (blood compensation) forms the basis of the Somali customary law for settlement of conflict between groups.

Other indigenous non-Somali communities include the Bravanese, mainly from the coastal towns of Brawa and Marka and Bajun and Tunnis of Bantu origin along the riverine areas. Small groups of non-indigenous communities such as Arabs, Indians and Pakistanis also live in Somalia, mainly in the large towns.

Minority Clans

A prime area of contention in Somali clan politics will concern the status and the fate of the so-called minority clans, particularly in the chaos of the civil war that has engulfed Somalia. As currently used by both Somalis and foreigners, the term 'minorities' refers to any clans or communities that do not belong genealogically to one of the four 'noble' clan families of Isaq, Darod, Hawiye and Dir. 'Noble', in this context, refers to the widespread Somali belief that members of the major clans are descendants of a common Somali ancestry and that the minority clans have a different – usually – mixed parentage, with Asian, Oromo or Bantu ancestors (Cassanelli, 1995a).

If one includes the agro-pastoral Rahanwein – clans of the riverine areas in the south – the minority clans make up one-third of the Somali population (Samater, 1991). However, due to their ancestral affiliation and shared tradition with major clan families as well as their relative numerical dominance in the Bay and Bakol regions in the south, the Rahanwein are generally classified along with the other major clan families (see, for example Lewis, 1988; Samater, 1991; Gilkes, 1994). The Rahanwien display their different identity in a number of ways, such as: speaking *Af Maay*, a regional dialect; mixed agro-economy; loss of genealogical continuity; mixed origin and attenuation of ancestral lineage. All these give grounds for prejudice and discrimination on the part of the 'noble' clans.

Most of the minorities live in relatively small, distinct communities throughout southern Somalia and often speak local dialects. They generally have distinctive features and tend to stand out physically because of their Bantu or Asiatic appearance. They are generally fishermen, farmers or artisans – occupations traditionally despised by their pasturalist compatriots. In Somaliland, there are a number of minority clans traditionally labelled as 'low caste'. Unlike the minority groups in the south, they neither speak distinct local dialects nor inhabit specific geographical areas. They follow so-called inferior occupations: Midgan (barbers and shoemakers); Tumal (blacksmiths) and Yibir (itinerants and peddlers). Most of the minority clans practise endogamy (marrying someone within their own or minority clans). In the Banaderi/Bravanese case marriage within the family is considered desirable in order to preserve their ethnic and cultural purity. However, in the case of other disadvantaged minority groups, it is often external cultural pressures that force the practice.

Under the Siad Barre regime, the diversity and very existence of minority groups was de-emphasised in an effort to present a homogenous country (Samater, 1991). Their political and social rights were grossly infringed. Until the civil war, minority groups seldom interacted and had no sense of political solidarity, but recently some have begun to perceive themselves as sharing 'second class' status and to consider themselves as minorities (Cassanelli, 1994). They suffered heavily from looting, intimidation and personal assaults in the militia battles that ravaged Somalia and especially the south. Despised by the warlords and largely unarmed and with no alliance, they have disproportionately been victims of the brutal civil war. Brawa, for example, has been devastated (Banafunzi, 1996) and many Bravanese fled the country.

Such raids are not random but sinister and calculated attempts to force them out of their traditional settlements by more powerful clans who coveted their lands. Though scarcely noted in media analysis, the fact is that the war in Somalia has essentially been a struggle over the country's resources – notably the rich farm lands in the south, and the export centres along the coast – mainly traditional homelands of the minority groups (Cassanelli, 1994).

The displacement of the minority clans is characterised not only by a change in geographical location but also a challenge to and potential loss of individual and group identity. Barring outside intervention or radical attitude change on the part of the perpetrators, it is unlikely that any minority group will ever be able to restore its corporate character within its traditional territories. They seem to have been left with no option other than to become a permanent class of refugees (Samater, 1991). Three of the most conspicuous minority groups in the country are now described:

The Benadiris

The Benadiris are long-term urban and generally prosperous communities who live in the ancient cities of Mogadishu (Hamar-weyn), Marka and Brawa along the Indian Ocean. The history of these cities goes back to the early 7th Century, when Arabs and Persians established trading posts along the Somali coast. The Benaderis, are distinct in their dialect and tradition. Traditionally, they are governed by councils of elders.

The *Reer* Hamar, as implicit in the word *reer* (group of people), are of cosmopolitan extraction, mainly of Asiatic origin, Yemenis in particular. The Yemeni connection is interesting as many Benadiri genealogies show Yemeni origin (Cassanelli, 1995b).

The Bravanese

The Bravanese (Barawanese), residents of the coastal city of Brawa, stand out as distinct ethnic group. They speak their own language, Cimini (or Bravanese), a dialect of Swahili, as their first language. They practice endogamy, marrying among themselves. Culturally, they belong more to the Swahili culture of East Africa than to the Cushitic culture of the Somalis (Samater, 1991). They still maintain their historical connections with the Swahili speaking communities in East Africa. This connection not only threw a life-line to displaced Bravanese, but also helped them in their settlement process following their displacement in the wake of civil war in Somalia.

Confusion has existed over the nationality of the growing Bravanese community in the UK. Since the majority arrived from Kenya, and speak Swahili rather than Somali as a mother tongue, the immigration authorities initially harboured suspicion that they were Kenyans exploiting the political turmoil in Somalia. However, families among the Bravanese communities in Waltham Forest and Newham have, according to Banafunzi (1996) expressed their anxiety that their children will not manage 'to settle into Bravanese society on their hoped for return'. Their specific Swahili dialect of Cimini (or Chimbalazi), confirms their Somali roots.

The Bantu

The Bantu groups live in the riverine areas of the Juba river. They are mainly farmers and artisans who had long been discriminated against by the mainstream pastoralists. The Bantu or Jareer (a reference to their 'African' features and hair texture) collectively known as Gosha (people of the bush) is a confederate of a number of distinct groups.

The Bantu are believed to be descendents of Negro slaves from East Africa. Historically, most of these groups have been clients of the dominant pastoral clans and have depended on them for protection and trade (Cassanelli, 1995b). The Bantus have also had similar relationships with the Benaderis and worked in their plantations as virtual slave labourers. Many of these groups have been partially Somalized. However, their historical low status vis-a-vis the Somalis and their recent suffering at the hands of armed militia have forced many to review their place in Somali society; some have even contemplated repatriating to their ancestral homelands in East Africa.

The current assertion of ethnic identities for all these minority groups has implications for the social interaction of their children with mainstream Somalis. This could have potential for quarrels or simple rivalry between the groups and may cause trouble in the classroom or the playground.

FACT FILE
* **Population**: 9,510,000.

* **Urban population**: 25%

* **Rural population**: 75%

* **Nationality**: Somali

* **Ethnic origin**: Hermitic stock

* **Ethnic divisions**: Somalis 90%, rest mainly Banaderi/Bravanese and Bantu; small groups of Asians and Europeans.

* **Physical characteristics**: Tall, slim-built with dark/brown complexion.

THE SOMALI FAMILY
Traditional Somali culture is based on a inherently unique social system. It is essentially egalitarian in nature and rooted in the traditional nomadic life-style. A typical nomadic encampment or an agricultural settlement may be described as a compact community of an autonomous family group, closely interconnected by numerous ties of common descent and marriage. Kinship is reckoned bilaterally, though it is predominantly patrilineal. Within traditional Somali society, the extended family is generally the norm.

The importance of the family
Kinship or blood ties are undoubtedly important in the clan-oriented Somali traditional relationship. In the absence of formal institutions, kinship ties matter most, constituting the primary form of social organisation. Family loyalty, however, is the predominant characteristic. This involves, on the one hand, the social obligation to put immediate family first and clan generally before others. On the other hand, in the critical and competitive environment, it entails the obligation to work for the well-being of the family. Traditionally, family and

by extension clan, take priority over individual preference. The individualism and independence so valued in the West appears selfish and irresponsible within the egalitarian spirit of the Somali society.

Adoption, mutual alliance or clientage, where a weak or persecuted person is taken into a household (a common practice among the Rahanwein community), do not necessary constitute a family or kinship in the Somali tradition.

Hierarchy in the family

Hierarchy in traditional Somali families is organised according to age and sex and crosses generations within an extended family system. Authority generally rests with males and older members; however, at macro level, it is clan elders who often hold greater public authority. Inherent in the patriarchal structure of the family, fathers generally assume a role as a head of the family. Their duty is to provide for their family, institute discipline and to maintain the unity, honour and social standing of the family. The mother who might appear to play a less important role, in reality commands considerable authority and respect within the nuclear family and beyond. Traditionally, Somali women are often forceful characters who may exercise more influence than appears on the surface (Lewis, 1993). The traditional roles of wives as homemakers and mothers and husbands of breadwinners still prevail, though they are beginning to give way to greater sharing and reduced segregation of tasks.

Relationships within the family

Relationships within the Somali family are close and dependent. They are relationships of loyalty, respect and obligation underpinning the duality enshrined in the family value system: parental love and affection; filial respect and obedience. The expectation placed upon the individual in a Somali family may seem unacceptable by Western standards. Indeed, the behaviour of the parents may seem enmeshed and intrusive. Mothers, for example, tend to have a great readiness to interest themselves in the affairs of their children. In the Somali tradition, the bond between mother and child is life long and unseverable. Sibling relationships are affectionate and emotional, often characterised by loyalty and interdependency. Friendship and social attachment are outwardly in nature, but generally occur within the confines of closer kin and neighbourhood. The inter-generation relationship is considered of paramount importance as the old and the young are uniquely combined within the family: age associated with wisdom and experience, and youth with vitality and hope.

Marriage and family organisation

Traditionally, Somali marriages were arranged between families. Marriage was considered as a contract between families, not just the two individuals. Indeed, matrimonial alliance plays an important role in the social and political life of Somali society. It is usually the man's family which takes the initiative in proposing marriage. The girl's family acts less directly, though parents and relatives of a marriageable girl are equally alert in the search of a suitable marriage. Elopement, though a common way to avoid such arranged matches, is considered as deviation and often rectified with the observance of some protocols to qualify for familial sanction. The urban trend towards allowing individuals to choose their own partners seems to affect marriage patterns in the interior (Lewis, 1993).

Somali marriage (in line with the *Shari'ah*) is basically a civil contract and its validity does not depend upon any religious ceremony or rites. However, the marriage contract *'meher'* is generally sanctioned by a sheikh or a religious person. The religious ceremony is left entirely to the Sheikh's discretion, and consequently there is no uniformity of ritual. The majority, though, follow the Prophet's traditional order.

Traditionally, the Somali marriage contract is not formalised in writing; however, its validity depends upon the consent of the parties, called *weydiin* and *guddoon* – 'declaration' and 'acceptance' – and the presence of witnesses. There should be an undertaking of settlement of an agreed value – in cash or kind – to be settled upon the wife. It is generally stipulated that the settlement should be held in reserve, to be paid to the wife in case of divorce against her will. The *meher* is usually followed by festive rejoicing of varying elaborateness and duration.

Marriage and family life are believed to be essential in the Somali tradition and are considered as a fulfilment of the tradition of the Prophet(s). As such, Somali marriage rests on spiritual authority. Single people are viewed as unfortunate and celibacy or monasticism, as an institution, are non-existent.

Polygamous marriages are still practised in Somalia, but there is a growing tendency towards monogamy. Marriage is extremely unstable with high divorce rates, particularly amongst the urban population. Factors such as public opinion, family pride and economic considerations, which have traditionally made the rupture of marital union difficult, seem to have either lost or changed their impact in the modern-day context. Being a divorcee is, however, often a temporary condition. Divorced men and women both have substantial rates of remarriage. One consequence of this is that a large number of female adults and children become part of step-families. With their distinctive emotional relationships among their members, such step-families have potential for far more frustration and breakdown.

RELIGION

Islam was brought to Somalia by Arabian missionaries and merchants who settled along the Somali coast in the 7th and 8th centuries. By the early 12th century, it had been spread through the hinterland by home missions. Well over 98% of the Somali people are Muslims of the Sunni sect. Islamic values are deeply rooted in the Somali identity and outlook. Indeed, being Somali is practically synonymous with being Muslim, though this does not necessarily have to be expressed by overtly pious behaviour. Somali law was traditionally based on *Sharia*, the Islamic moral and legal code, and even with the introduction of secular power, Islamic jurisdiction has retained much influence.

As Muslims, Somalis are expected to live according to the *Qur'an* and *Sunnah* – the practices of the Prophet. Accordingly, they have to observe all religious obligations and celebrate all the major Muslim festivals.

Every action taken with the awareness that it fulfils the will of Allah is considered as an act of worship in Islam. Nevertheless, the specific acts of worship, termed the Pillars of Islam, provide the framework of spiritual life.

The Five Pillars of Islam are:

- *Shahada* – declaration of faith.

- *Salat* – prayer, five times a day at appointed times

- *Zakat* – almsgiving or charity.

- *Saum* – fasting during the month of Ramadan.

- *Hajj* – pilgrimage to Makkah, at least once in one's life time, if possible.

The Main Festivals are:

- *Eid ul-Fitr* – 'The Festival of Breaking the Fast'. This festival takes place each year immediately at the end ofthe month of Ramadan Celebrations usually go on for three days.

- *Eid ul-Adhha* – 'The Festival of Sacrifice'. This festival begins on the tenth day of the month of Dul-Haja in the Islamic calendar. It is a festival of thanksgiving for those who completed the Hajj or pilgrimage in Makkah. The festivities usually go on for three more days.

- *Mawlid Al-Nabi* – 'The Birth of the Prophet'. This is celebrated on the twelfth of the third month in the Islamic calendar. In fact, the whole month is celebrated as the birth of the prophet.

- *Hijra* – 'The Migration – journey of the Prophet to Medina'. This day marks the beginning of the Islamic calendar. It is celebrated on the first of Muharram.

It is important to note that the Islamic Festivals are based on the Lunar Calendar so it is not possible to give exact dates for these festivals. They do not relate to the Western calendar.

Dietary Laws
Somalis, like other Muslims, are permitted to eat only food that conforms to Islamic law. The *Qur'an* (Muslim holy book) ordered certain food to be '*haram*' – forbidden. Unlawful food includes:

- any product of the pig: bacon, ham, lard, etc.

- any meat containing blood

- any flesh eating animal

- any animal strangled, beaten to death or killed by a fall

- any animal sacrificed to idols.

Somalis are allowed to eat meat, but only when slaughtered in the Islamic way. This means the animal's throat is slit in one cut, while the name of Allah is invoked. This is known as '*halal*'. Somalis, along with other faithful Muslims, are not also allowed to drink alcohol or eat any food that contains or is prepared with alcohol. (See also chapter 5: Religion and Somali Children).

Dress Code

Like food, Islam has a strict rule about what people wear – and what they do not wear! Islam considers dress a basic human requirement. Both men and women are, therefore, expected to dress modestly.

Men are not supposed to wear silk or gold, which would make them vain. They can be bare-chested, if necessary; but they should make sure they are covered from waist to knee.

In some Muslim countries, women wear a veil which almost covers the face. The wearing of the veil is not, however, a religious obligation; rather it is a tradition. In the Somali tradition rooted as it is in the Islamic culture, women should not wear tight or see-through clothes. Clothes should cover the whole body and their hair should be covered by a scarf.

LOCAL CUSTOM

The core values and practices in Islam are derived from the Qur'an and the Traditions of the Prophet. The prevalent environmental and cultural factors, however, tend to give separate character and identities to nations in the different parts of the Islamic world. Somalis are Sunni Muslims of the Shafi'i sect and are divided into three main denominations: the Qaderia, Ahmedia and the Salihia. These denominations (*Dariqo*) generally manifest minor differences of ritual and interpretation of the Sharia.

A complementary relationship is seen between laity and the man of God, traditionally expressed in the phrase *wadaad iyo waranleh* (Lewis, 1993). Sheikhs or priests are traditionally highly regarded and held in the greatest respect, if not reverence. Apart from their formal religious roles of solemnising marriages, officiating at funerals and leading prayers, some sheikhs are known for their religious miracles in curing the sick. These remarkable cures are often attributed to their subtle intercession and many sheikhs are particularly sought after for their holy writ amulet and potions.

Reputed saints (*awliyo*) are not very numerous in Somalia, but are believed to possess special powers of blessing. Historically, some religious leaders, for example Sheikh Yussuf Al-Kownein (*Aw Barkhadleh*), obtained a great reputation for sanctity and ascetic life before their death. Shrines were often erected as a sign of devout reverence after their death, thus establishing a saintly reputation for the departed spiritual leader. It is not unusual for the followers of a particular saint to make regular pilgrimage to the shrine. Ancestor veneration remains important in certain traditional circles.

The Somali people generally manifest a philosophical perspective on life based on their belief of *Qadar* – fate or predestination. On the one hand, this outlook has a cushioning effect on the mishaps and mis-fortunes of life; on the other hand, it predisposes a somewhat fatalistic attitude to life. However, this is less apparent in the practice of the educated sections of the community, who generally adopt a more prag-matic realism in life.

A different order
The Muslim communities in Britain come predominantly from the Indian sub-continent and the Middle East. These communities are fairly well established in Britain and generally have the resources to practise their religion and maintain their Islamic ethos. Moreover, the shared linguistic and cultural framework within each of these main communities further provide opportunities for support and collabora-tion (see Parker-Jenkins, 1995).

The Somalis generally lack the resources necessary to establish their own religious centres to suit their linguistic and cultural dimension. They often find themselves in limbo, feeling at best sidelined by the more established Muslim communities (see El-Sohl, 1991). In the East end of London, where there is a community, Somali faithfuls often share facilities with the predominant Bengali community, whose practices and ceremonies differ from theirs. For instance, they worship in mosques where the imams deliver the Friday sermon in Bengali.

Despite ranking among the oldest settled migrant groups in Britain's Dockland areas, the Somalis still continue to struggle for a fairer share of scarce resources. Sheikh Omer, a Somali religious scholar in Greenwich, laments the lack of religious buildings exclusive to the Somali community, where they could get together for daily prayer and other religious functions. Muslim communities who are themselves struggling for survival in Britain can hardly offer any significant finan-cial or material support to their Somali 'brethren'.

NAMING SYSTEM

Somalis use a mixture of traditional Somali and Islamic naming systems. They have a first personal name, followed by their father's personal name, then that of the grandfather. Usually, a Somali is known by the combination of these three names. Thus, Musa Ali Abdi mean: Musa, who is the son of Ali and grandson of Abdi. Nicknames are quite common and form part of a personal or family identity. Women keep their own names after marrying.

In Western countries, many Somalis adopt their grandfather's name as a family name; but there are many instances when the father's name is used as a family name. Even so, some women do not always assume their husbands' family name.

The orthographic representation of some Somali names may occasionally pose difficulties. A Somali name with an Arabic origin may have assumed a local identity with slightly modified pronunciation. One person may use a name of this kind in its present Somali form, while another may refer back to its original Arabic form. Slight phonetic variation, enough to cause some confusion, would occur when transliterated into English.

For example:

Maryam – The Arabic form

Maryan – The Somali-ized form. (*The Somali phonological system does not permit final 'm'*).

Mariam or Marian – English spelling.

Therefore it is important to check the names against official documentation to avoid confusion. Another issue of some concern is the correct pronunciation of Somali names. Teachers should ask parents and Somali teachers for help with the correct pronunciation and do their best to get it right. Anglicising Somali names can be wholly unacceptable.

ECONOMY

The economy is largely agricultural, dependent upon nomadic stock-raising in the north and irrigated plantation farming in the south around the Shabelle and Juba rivers. About 70% of the working population is employed in the agriculture sector. Livestock, skin and hides are the main exports. The major cash crops are banana and sugar cane. Subsistence crops include sorghum and maize. Processing raw materials constitute the bulk of the small industry.

The most valuable mineral resource is uranium; many other minerals are largely unexploited. Petroleum deposits have been found; but it is not yet known (at least officially) whether they warrant commercial exploitation. American petroleum companies were granted exploration rights but suspended investigation following the civil war. Somalia's coastal and offshore seas have considerable potential for fisheries but this industry is relatively undeveloped. Historically, fishing had been of little significance to the economy as a whole as well as to the traditional dietary habits of the Somali people, who prefer meat.

The Somali economy was damaged by a combination of wide-spread corruption, a severe drought in 1974, war with Ethiopia in 1977-78, and has lately been devastated by war. In the absence of a government-initiated economic plan, an unconventional economy regulated by individual businessmen and fuelled by remittance money from abroad has recently evolved. Returns from expatriate workers in Gulf states still remains an important source of income. In Somaliland, the 'government' started to exploit the economic potential of the country and introduced tax, banking and customs systems. However, the recent disturbances in Hargeisa and Burao and the lack of international recognition have halted the momentum, resulting in setbacks for the recovery of the economy.

FACT FILE

- **Agriculture**: Dominant sector – 65% of GDP pastoral nomads.
- **Livestock Raising**: 45% OF GDP
- **Crop Production**: 10% OF GDP
- **Industries**: A few small industries, mainly in agricultural processing.
- **Mineral Resources**: few commercially viable minerals.
- **Fishery**: Potentially rich but largely unexploited.
- **Major Exports**: Bananas, livestock, fish, hides and skins.
- **Major Cash Crops**: bananas, sugar cane.
- **Subsistence Crops**: sorghum, maize.
- **Mode of Living**: 75% lead nomadic mode of living

EDUCATION

Education is poorly developed and at present practically non-existent in many areas. The civil war that engulfed Somalia has deprived all children of formal education. In Somaliland, the goverment has so far opened a number of primary schools. Further south, UNICEF has somehow succeeded in re-establishing primary schools in big towns. Most buildings are still derelict, with little basic furniture and equipment. Teachers are in short supply and often work for little or no wages. There are, however, some adequately resourced private schools in these towns. Further south, local committees of elders, teachers and parents have setup rudimentary classes on a self-help basis and have so far reintroduced basic education. *Malcaamado (Qur'anic* schools) are also in operation, mainly through charitable ventures.

Formal education is a recent development in Somalia. Traditionally, Somali education consisted primarily of teaching the *Qur'an* and other aspects of the Islamic religion. Such provision was never universal but confined to a small urban minority. For the bulk of the nomadic population, the spoken word was intensively cultivated as the main medium for transmitting cultural norms and moral values. Habits and skills were also acquired through parental stewardship and exposure to adult life.

In the earlier colonial period, the Somalis strongly resisted the introduction of Western-type education; it was only after World War I that the Somalis permitted colonial powers to open schools. The colonial education system was limited in all intents and purposes to a small cadre for administrative and clerical work. In British Somaliland, education was based on the British model with English as the medium of instruction, while in the south, Italian was the medium.

Great strides were made after independence in the expansion of primary education. However, the colonial legacy remained in place with the two different educational systems in operation, to be unified only in 1963. However, the respective mediums of instruction were left in place: Arabic/ English in the North and Italian in the South. A unified curriculum and an eight-year period of primary level education was adopted.

Important and radical changes took effect when the military government came to power in late 1969. In 1972 all private schools became nationalised and free and compulsory primary education was introduced. In the same year, the military regime declared Somali the sole official language. As a result, both English and Italian were withdrawn totally from the education system, except as subjects among others at the secondary level. In 1974, the government launched the Rural Development campaign, which was basically designed to extend literacy among the rural population. (This is further discussed under see Language in Chaper 4).

Secondary education facilities were limited to the major cities and towns. Even before the total collapse of the education system, following the all-out civil war, schools were poverty-stricken: school buildings in poor condition, classes very large, books and equipment in short supply. Teaching methods were formal, underpinned by strict discipline and considerable reliance on rote learning. Laboratories and workshops were too poorly equipped to allow much opportunity for pupils to do practical work. Entry to a standard or form does not necessarily depend on age. A child should in theory start school at the age of six but may not begin in school until the age of about nine or ten. As a result, it is not unusual for a class to contain children of widely varying ages.

The Siad Barre government placed little premium on education, eroding public confidence in its value. The teaching profession has lost its differential status and works in makeshift conditions with little pay or regard for its protests.

Whereas attempts are being made to re-establish primary education, higher education had completely collapsed. The Somali National University, which had over 8,000 students in the early 1990s, was closed in 1992. Armed soldiers and militia men stormed the university and looted everything they could move. The National University used Italian as the medium of instruction. Only the Faculty of Education at Lafole and the National Polytechnic used English.

There is a gender gap at all levels, with the disparity more marked in higher education as many girls drop out to settle into married life. So far more women than men are illiterate, reflecting the difference in gender roles and status.

There was an inept, fragmented language policy which failed to take advantage of Somalia's linguistic homogeneity. Even the official status accorded to Somali and Arabic did not help towards codifying a long-term efficient language policy. From the Qur'anic school to university, one was expected to find one's way through the maze of different languages: Arabic, Somali, English and Italian! This inept, politically motivated language policy has resulted in major problems in the education system, thus contributing to the poor educational standard.

The education system in the UK is very different and therefore can present many Somali children with certain difficulties. Such children will take time to adjust to the new learning environment and the methodology commonly employed in the UK (see Experience at School in Chapter 6).

FACT FILE

- **Education System**: Three levels: elementary, intermediate and secondary, each lasting for four years.

- **Medium of Instruction**: Somali

- **Entry into Education System**: standard or form

- **Teaching Method**: formal, disciplined and teacher-centred.

- **Age of Compulsory Education**: 6-16

- **Other Languages**: Arabic and English.

Chapter 2

HISTORICAL AND POLITICAL BACKGROUND

HISTORICAL AND POLITICAL INFORMATION

Somalia is associated with a long and turbulent history. To the ancient Egyptians, it was known as the 'Land of Punt', from where frankincense and myrrh were brought to grace the Pharaonic temples in the 15th century BC. Phoenician traders called Somalia the 'region of incense'. Greek and Roman traders were also familiar with the region and called the land 'Cape Aromatica' and the people Berbers (hence the port town on the Gulf of Aden named Berbera).

The origins of the Somali people have been traced back into the first millennium AD when northern Somali clans began to migrate northwards to the Horn of Africa (Lewis, 1993; Laitin, 1992), probably pasturalist nomads in search of grazing for their herds. In the 7th century, Muslim Arabs and Persians began to arrive on Somalia's shores on trading expeditions. Immigrant missionaries settled in ports along the coasts and brought Islamic culture in the 9th and 10th centuries, adding to the cultural mosaic in the cities of Mogadishu, Merca and Brawa in the south and Zeila and Berbera in the North. Soon centres of Islamic and Arabic scholarship flourished in all Somali towns, initiating a new zest for religious evangelism. In the 15th and 16th centuries, Somali warriors took part in the 'holy war' against Ethiopia led by Ahmed Garan (or Ahmed 'Gurey' – the left-handed – as he was better known by Somalis). In the first detailed reference in written chronicle to Somali people, these warriors were described as being especially expert at road ambushes (Lewis, 1993). From the 17th to 19th centuries, stretches of Somali southern coasts became sultanates, controlled by Arab rulers of first Muscat and later Zanzibar.

In the early 19th century the Horn of Africa began to attract colonial interests because of its strategic location on the Red Sea. In the scramble for the division of Africa, following the Berlin Conference in 1884, the northern part of Somalia became a British Protectorate and the south an Italian colony. France annexed the part that became Djibouti. In 1897, the Reserved Areas of Somaliland were ceded to Ethiopia under the Anglo-Abysinian Treaty. The subsequent period of turmoil culminated in the nationalist struggle against the colonial powers led by Sayid Mohammed Abdullah Hassan (1900-1920).

In 1936 Somaliland was temporarily incorporated into Italian East Africa, but in 1941 it was recaptured by a British counter-offensive which also forced the Italians to withdraw from Eritrea, Italian Somalia and Ethiopia. In 1950, Italian Somalia was returned to Italy as UN trust territory for ten years. Nationalistic and pan-Somali sentiment erupted in Somaliland and eventually forced Britain to grant it independence.

INDEPENDENCE AND UNITY 1960
Somalia achieved independence from the British and the Italians in 1960. Soon after, the former British Protectorate in the North and the Italian colony in the South united to form the Somali Republic. Somalia's first president was Aden Abdulah Osman. He was succeeded in June 1967 by Abdirashid Ali Sharmarke who appointed a cabinet led by Mohamed Ibrahim Egal. The relationship between the two regions, however, has always been a dangerous balance of economic and political power. While the South might have succeeded in retaining political precedence, the North has accumulated considerable wealth and achieved high standards of education. However, the economic power and professional potential of the North was clearly dispro-portionate to their political power. This imbalance was a prelude to a process of polarisation that led to the eventual disintegration of Somalia.

THE DISINTEGRATION OF SOMALIA
For almost a decade since Independence, Somalia was led by successive civilian governments and the country enjoyed parliamentary democracy with relative stability. Freedom of speech, assembly and association were considered an integral part of the democratic process. The multi-party system, however, gave way to political confusion as clans vied with each other to form their own political parties. This

culminated in a highly politicised and divisive election in early 1969 in which over 60 parties contested 120 seats. On 15 October 1969, President Abdirashid Ali Sharmarke was assassinated by a police officer, signalling a political upheaval.

BARRE IN POWER

On 21 October 1969, General Barre seized power in a military coup. Parliament was abolished, the constitution was suspended and a military council took over. Soon after, Siad Barre proclaimed his intention of breaking the clan system and introducing a fair political system. However, under the banner of Marxist socialism, he created a system of state control by terror and oppression (*Africa Watch*, 1990).

Somalia forged a strong alliance with the then Soviet Union in the early 1960s and was among the first Black African states to allow the Soviets to establish a strong foothold in the geo-politically strategic Horn of Africa. When the military junta came to power, the military and economic ties were so strengthened that Somalia was dubbed a 'soviet satellite'. It boasted the strongest military force in Black Africa (Gilkes, 1994).

In a desperate effort to divert attention from internal popular dissent, Siad Barre played his nationalist trump card and ordered the armed forces to invade Ethiopia in 1977. Siad Barre's military incursion was initially successful, but soon turned disastrous when the Soviet Union switched alliance and sided with Ethiopia. The Soviet Union provided dozens of planes and hundreds of tanks to Ethiopia and arranged for nearly 20,000 troops from their close ally Cuba to help drive the Somalis out in an Ethiopian counter-offensive in February 1978 (Gilkes, 1994). Somalia abrogated its treaty of friendship with the Soviet Union and improved its relations with the West and the Arab world. In 1980 Barre's regime granted air and naval facilities to the US in exchange for military and economic assistance.

One aftermath of the military incursion was the influx of refugees fleeing from war and famine. The war and the subsequent border conflict in the 1980s resulted in a huge refugee crisis in the region, as ethnic Somalis fled the Ethiopian counter incursion and famine. Somalia claimed that ethnic Somalis were systematically expelled from the Ogaden; Ethiopia contested by saying they were welcome to stay if loyal to the government. In early 1981, there were an estimated 1.3 million refugees in camps and more than 20,000 scattered in cities and towns.

After defeat in the war, followed by an abortive coup, Siad Barre instigated desperate and repressive measures. The Majeerten clan was first to be targeted, for their backing of the *coup d''etat*. An agressive course of scorched earth policy then fell on the main northern clan – the Isaq. These measures resulted in the formation of armed opposition groups such as the Somali Salvation Democratic Front (SSDF) and, in 1981, the Somali National Movement (SNM).

THE OPPOSITION MOVEMENTS

In 1988, the SNM launched a general offensive against the military bases in the northern towns of Burao and Hargeisa. The military government responded by indiscriminate shelling and aerial bombard-ment of Burao and Hargeisa. Hargeisa was literally razed to the ground and thousands of civilians lost their lives. Well over 400,000 people were forced to flee the country, mainly into squalid refugee camps in neighbouring Ethiopia, with 45,000 in Djibouti.

In early January 1991, the Somali United Congress (USC), backed mainly by the Hawiye clan, marched into Mogadishu. An immediate public uprising followed in which Siad Barre forces were defeated after four weeks of fierce fighting in the capital and fled south to the Gedo region, his clan base. The USC named Ali Mahdi Mohamed interim president and invited other opposition groups to negotiate a new government in a national conference. The SNM and other opposition movements declined to join. The SNM formed an administration to govern the former territory of Somaliland.

THE NORTH PROCLAIMS INDEPENDENCE

In May 1991, the SNM restored the sovereignty of Somaliland and formed a government of the Somaliland Republic. Abdirahman Ahmed Ali, chairman of the SNM, was elected president. Since the SNM carried out no acts of retribution there was a spell of stability, whereas southern Somalia was riven by civil war (Drysdale, 1991). There was no international recognition, however, and Somaliland did not receive aid to restore the crumbled economy. Economic and political stagnation created an atmosphere of mistrust and polarisation. Sub-clan rivalry within the Isaq led in 1992 to fighting between rival factions of the army in the towns of Buroa and Berbera. A reconciliation committee of elders initiated peace talks and the fighting ceased – but not without grudges and animosity.

Somaliland in 1997 has a civilian government headed by Mohamed Ibrahim Egal, a former prime minister of Somalia, serving his second term in office. The administration has made some progress in rebuilding the infrastructure and has proved overall to be successful in rebuilding a judicial system, civil order as well as hospitals and schools. Serious disturbances, however, erupted in Hargeisa and Buroa in early 1995. Again elders initiated peace talks, and hostilities now seem suspended.

CIVIL WAR IN MOGADISHU

The spiralling civil war in southern Somalia has its roots in the USC's inability to form a viable alternative following the collapse of Barre's regime. In June 1991, a major rift within the USC was reported, with factional rivalry between two Hawiye sub-clans, led by Ali Mahdi and General Aidid. On mid November, Aidid's faction launched a full-scale attack on Ali Mahdi's position in the capital and captured most of the city. Ali Mahdi's Abgal militia were driven out but soon regained control of much of the north of Mogadishu. More than 4,000 people, mostly civilians, were killed and well over 20,000 wounded in the factional fighting (Laitin, 1992). As the conflict intensified, Ali Mahdi appealed to the UN for intervention. Aidid initially opposed any UN mission in Somalia, but in August 1991 he finally agreed to the deployment of 500 UN troops to escort food to alleviate the severe famine affecting many parts of the country.

A cease-fire in March 1992 was organised by the United Nations, but both leaders regarded this as temporary and made efforts to find other clan allies. After the deployment of the peacekeeping troops, the UN began to play a more active role, but there were disputes over the control and size of the force and ultimately their special envoy resigned, maintaining that the UN mishandled the whole operation and was grossly incompetent in the organisation and execution of the relief and peacekeeping operation and that it failed to take a grassroots approach and support local community leaders and the NGOs rather the warlords (Sahnuon, 1992).

OPERATION RESTORE HOPE

In December 1992, the Security Council sanctioned a proposal by the US to establish a secure environment for humanitarian operations in Somalia. An advance contingent of 1800 US Marines landed at Mogadishu and took control of the port and seaport. The US members of the Unified Task Force (UNITAF) were reinforced with a multi-national force drawn from 21 countries. Operation Restore Hope rapidly established control over much of the south and security and food deliveries were much improved. UNITAF's intention to bring a rapprochement between the hostile factions failed, however, leading to an armed clash between UNITAF and General Aidid's militia.

Eventually, UNITAF reduced its forces in Somalia and in May 1993 turned over control to UNOSOM II. In June, a clash between a Pakistani UN unit and Aidid's militia left 35 Pakistanis and many Somalis dead. The UN condemned the action as unprovoked and ordered Aidid's arrest. A chain reaction of attack and counter attack left scores of UN soldiers including a dozen US Delta Force and hundreds of Somalis dead in a battle in Mogadishu in October, 1993 (Luling, 1995). With the increase of US casualties, President Clinton announced March 1994 as the date for the withdrawal of US ground forces in Somalia, later to be followed by a complete UN withdrawal in March 1995. In February 1995, Aidid and Ali Mahdi signed a truce to stop the clan-based fighting, but with little success.

THE CURRENT SITUATION

In early June, 1996, Aidid's leadership of the USC was challenged by Osman Ato, his former key supporter and financier. General Aidid nominated himself as the new president of Somalia. Mahdi responded by forming an alliance with Ato and a dangerous new phase of intra-clan fighting began. Aidid was hit by gunfire as he fought for control of Mogadishu and died on August 1, 1996. Aidid's death was expected to break the impasse, but Aidid's son, a former US marine, stepped into his father's shoes as 'interim president', rejected offers of cease-fire and negotiations by rival clans and opted to continue the cycle of death and destruction.

At the start of 1997, Ali Mahdi was still 'interim president' and chair-man of the Somali Salvation Alliance (SSA). There have been reports of widespread starvation and malnutrition, especially among children and the elderly, following a new and fierce wave of factional fighting. Somaliland continues struggling to gain international recognition since reclaiming independence in 1991.

Somalia is far from a stable country. Thousands are already in neighbouring countries as refugees; many others are internally displaced. A small proportion have made their way out to seek asylum elsewhere, mainly in Europe and North America, or are living in the Gulf states.

CHRONOLOGY

15th C. BC	Ancient Egyptians call at Somali ports to collect incense.
7th to 10th C.	Muslim Arabs and Persians establish trading posts along Somali coast.
15/16th C.	Ahmed Garan joined Arab sultanates in their battle with Ethiopia
1884-87	British protectorate of Somaliland established.
1889	Italian colony of Somalia established.
1897	Reserved Areas (the Ogaden) of Somaliland ceded to Ethiopia.
1900-1920	The Dervish movement led by Sayid Mohammed Abdullah Hassan.
1936	Somaliland temporarily incorporated into Italian East Africa.
1941	Somaliland recaptured by a British counter-offensive.
1950	Italian Somalia returned to Italy as UN trust territory.
1960	Independence and unification to form Somali Republic.
1969	President Sharmarkeh assassinated. Siad Barre seized power in a military coup; parliament abolished; constitution suspended.
1970	Siad Barre declared Somalia a socialist state.

1977/78	Eight-month war with Ethiopia. Somali forces repulsed with Soviet and Cuban assistance.
1978	Popular discontent and armed insurrection led to an abortive *coup d'etat* by the Majerteen clan.
1982	Somali National Movement (SNM) formed.
1988	SNM launched military offensive in the northern towns. Counter measures by Siad Barre forces; Hargeisa and Burao destroyed.
1989	Hawiye clan drawn into popular insurrection.
Feb. 1991	Mogadishu captured by Somali United Forces (USC). Barre fled to Gedo region. Ali Mahdi appointed interim president.
May 1991	SNM restored sovereignty of Somaliland June 1991 – major rift reported within USC.
Sept. 1991	Factional fighting in Mogadishu. Thousands of casualties reported. Mahdi appealed for UN intervention.
Nov. 1992	UNOSOM secured Mogadishu airport but relief operations severely hindered. UN peace keeping troops led by US Marines sent in to protect relief operations.
May 1993	UNITAF reduced its forces and handed over to UNOSOM II
Feb. 1994	Ali Mahdi and Aidid sign truce to stop clan-based fighting.
March 1994	Western peace-keeping troops withdrawn.
May 1995	Complete UN withdrawal. Clan-based fighting continues.
June, 1996	Aidid and Aato fall out.
August, 1996	Aidid dies. Succeeded by his son, Hussein Aidid.
December, 1996	Factional fighting in Mogadishu claims many civilian lives.
February, 1997	Egal elected to serve second term as President.

Chapter 3

THE SOMALI COMMUNITY IN THE UK

Somalis are believed to have first come to Britain in the late 19th century (Little, 1948; Collins, 1957). Most Somalis – migrants and refugees – in the UK are from Somaliland, though refugees arriving lately are also from the South.

The early Somali migrants were predominantly male, working in the Royal or Merchant Navy. Most settled in the docklands of London and Cardiff, a few in Liverpool, Hull, Bristol and other ports. After the end of each World War, demobilised soldiers joined them. By the end of the 1950s, the economic boom in Britain coupled with decreasing job opportunities in the Merchant Navy, encouraged more Somalis to seek employment outside the seafaring industry and to settle in industrial centres such as Sheffield and Manchester.

A large number of migrant Somalis arrived in the early 1960s when the men brought over their spouses and children. In London, they settled in the East End near their jobs in the booming docks where they were easily accommodated by the local community and economy. This community was relatively well established, with a strong sense of its own identity and self-sufficiency but the severe decline of the British Merchant Navy and the economic recession in the early 1970s have drastically affected employment.

Somalis who came in the 1980s did so not for economic reasons but because of political persecution, civil war and fear for their lives. The first wave of refugees were predominantly from middle class backgrounds; later, more vulnerable people arrived to seek asylum.

There are now an estimated 60,000 Somalis in Britain. The highest concentration is in Tower Hamlets, Newham and Ealing. In some London boroughs, the Somali community is the largest or second largest ethnic group.

REFUGEE EXPERIENCE AND SETTLEMENT PROBLEMS

Perhaps the most important factor in the settlement process of the Somalis is the refugee experience. Adjusting to life in a new environment is difficult, even under optimum conditions. It is much easier to adjust to a situation if it is of one's choosing but Somali refugees have been driven out of their country by the political turmoil and civil war.

Somalis do not arrive in the UK as part of a sponsorship programme like the Vietnamese, Chileans or more recently the Bosnians do. Such resettlement schemes usually provide provisional reception centres for acclimatisation and orientation and may also offer services such as language instruction, job training and even some starting capital and may also include an appropriate induction programme for school-age children.

Somalis, however, generally arrive on an *ad hoc* basis and with varied experience en route to Britain. The majority flee Somalia to a transit country where they try to get a visitor or student visa or one for family reunion. Some who do not have proper documents try to obtain papers on the black market, often at extortionate prices. A few people come for family reunion but for most seeking asylum is the sole objective.

APPLYING FOR ASYLUM

People who have no proper documents immediately go to the immigration officers who deal with their requests for asylum. A short interview is generally given to establish the authenticity of their claim. Those who convince the immigration authorities are allowed in on Temporary Admission while the Home Office considers their application; others are sent to detention centres for further investigation.

The great majority who go through immigration control in some other formal capacity apply for asylum, usually within one week of entering the UK. Recent legislation decrees that people who apply for asylum after arriving in the country are no longer entitled to income support or housing benefit (see Asylum Bill).

When a Somali has applied for asylum, his/her status is that of **asylum-seeker**. An asylum-seeker can be defined as: 'a person who has crossed an international border to seek safety and refugee status' (Rutter, 1994). The average waiting time for applications is currently eight months. There are three possible decisions: refugee status is refused; refugee status is refused *but* exceptional leave to remain (ELR) is granted; or refugee status is granted.

Six months after applying, an asylum-seeker can write to the Home Office to ask for a variation of his/her conditions of stay to take up employment. Asylum-seekers are entitled to 90% of basic Income Support until they have been accepted by the Home Office.

Children under 16 have an entitlement to education irrespective of immigration status or length of stay; however, Somali asylum-seekers who wish to go to college full-time will find that they have to pay the overseas student fee – an amount far beyond their humble means. They are not entitled to a student grant until they have completed 3 years ordinary residence, whereupon they become a home student. Meanwhile, they can only attend a part-time course that is within the 21-hour limit or they forfeit benefit.

These rules restrict the chances of asylum-seekers desperate to continue their studies after years of disruption. Somali asylum-seeking students have so far been able to have their fees waived for English and other short courses but the Asylum and Immigration Bill will possibly prevent even these studies.

As the chart below demonstrates, the number of Somalis recognised as refugees and granted asylum has fallen sharply to less than 1% in 1995. In the 1990s, the great majority are no longer recognised as refugees but granted ELR and the number of refusals has increased markedly.

year	application	refugee status	ELR	refusal
1989	1,850	815	260	10
1990	2,250	275	75	25
1991	1,995	50	225	40
1992	1,575	25	2,221	320
1993	1,465	45	3,075	210
1994	1,840	5	1,575	150
1995	3,465	10	2,205	185

Source: Home Office Statistics, June, 1995

Over the last ten years, asylum policy in the UK has steadily become more restrictive. At the same time as the Asylum Act was passed, there were changes in immigration rules which in effect tightened the criteria by which an asylum application is being judged. In the two years prior to the introduction of the Act, only 16% of all decisions were refusals, compared with over 75% in the 1990s. Only 5% now receive full refugee status, with some 20% being offered ELR.

The Home Office contends that the majority of Somalis are technically 'displaced' people. People who are exiled because of war or disaster do not necessarily meet the definition of the UN Convention relating to the status of refugees. So the overwhelming majority of Somalis are deemed not to qualify for refugee status. They may, however, be granted ELR at the discretion of the Home Secretary on grounds that it is not safe for them to return home.

Under International Law, the word refugee has precise meaning. However, in everyday speech the term is used more generally to include also those applying for asylum and those granted ELR and, unless otherwise specified, it is used in this way throughout the book.

A refugee is defined in Article 1 of the UN Convention Relating to the Status of Refugees 1951 (the 'Geneva Convention') and the Protocol Relating to the Status of Refugees 1967 as: someone who, *'owing to well-founded fear of being persecuted for reasons of race, religion, nationality, membership of a particular social group or political opinion'* has fled his country or is unable to return to it.

In 1969, the Organisation of African Unity (OAU) broadened their definition of a refugee to include those who have been forced to leave their home country as result of *'external aggression or domination, occupation, foreign domination or events seriously disturbing public order.'*

More than 120 countries are signatories to the UN Geneva Convention and are legally bound to honour its obligations. There are, however, a number of developing countries that seem to lack the proper legal, social or economic framework to fully accommodate the needs of refugees. It is the task of the UN High Commissioner for Refugees to ensure that these countries respect their obligations.

At present, only a handful of Somalis are recognised as refugees. Those granted asylum will be given leave to remain for four years, followed by permanent residence. They also have the right to work and to use health and social services. To pursue further or higher education, a Somali refugee can either apply for a grant or pay fees at the home student rate.

Children born outside the UK and married partners of Somali refugees will be given status and have the same rights as refugees. Somali children born in the UK after January, 1983 have no automatic right to British citizenship unless at least one parent is British or has permanent residence in the UK at the time of the child's birth. However, if at least one parent becomes British or is lawfully settled (i.e. indefinite leave), s/he can then be registered as British.

Somalis granted ELR can remain in the UK initially for one year. This is usually followed by two renewals of leave of three years each. Towards the end of the seven years, they can apply for indefinite leave (permanent residence). Children and married partners of a Somali with ELR status will be granted the same status and rights as their parent/ partner. If a Somali child remains in the UK for 10 years after his/her birth, s/he will be entitled to register as British, irrespective of the status of his/her parents.

Somalis who have ELR can work, though in practice, they rarely get into proper employment. Somali children who finish school find it difficult to study at college or university as they have to satisfy the three-year residence criteria to qualify for a mandatory grant or pay fees at the home student rate.

FAMILY REUNION

'Family' is defined by the Home Office as a group consisting of or two parents and dependent children only and excludes other relations. So it recognises only the nuclear rather than the extended family pattern that pertains in Somalia.

The procedure for family reunion for Somalis is complicated by the unfolding human tragedies in the region. Following the war in the North in early 1988, the Home Office introduced a special arrangement for family reunion as a humanitarian gesture.

Alongside the normal procedure whereby the partner or dependent children can apply to the nearest British Embassy, an application could be submitted on their behalf direct to the Home Office in the UK. This special arrangement was extended to asylum-seekers and people granted ELR and extended family were also considered for reunion.

With tighter immigration control measures now in place, the normal procedure for family reunion is strictly back in place. This means that a single application can be made by the main asylum-seeker for the whole family only if the family is in the UK at the time of the application. Otherwise family reunion will be conditional on the immigration status of the main applicant.

Where refugee status has been granted, an application can be made by the Somali refugee to the Home Office and by the partner/dependent children to the nearest British Embassy for family reunion. Somalis who have been granted ELR cannot be joined for four years after the decision, unless they can prove that they can support and accommodate their family without recourse to public funding – a condition rarely met due to their dire financial situation. The Home Office, however, do occasionally permit family reunion on compassionate grounds.

A Somali asylum-seeker has no automatic right to family reunion while awaiting decision on the application.

THE ASYLUM AND IMMIGRATION BILL 1996

The Bill amends and supplements the Immigration Act (1971) and the Asylum and Immigration Appeals Act (1993). The new measures will affect the social and economic circumstances of asylum-seekers and refugees.

Social Security changes which came into force in February 1996 will deny benefit to new Somali asylum-seeker unless they apply for status as they enter the country. Those who put in a claim to remain in the UK while already in the country, rather than at the port of entry, or who appeal against a refusal decision will no longer be entitled to Income Support, Housing Benefit or any non-contributory benefits.

Research conducted by the Refugee Council early in 1996 showed that 80% of its clients make in-country applications within the first week of arrival. A relatively large number of Somalis are among those who apply after entry to the UK as they are not sure of the procedure. Moreover, many are traumatised by the political upheaval and civil war in their home country and generally feel apprehensive least the decision be negative and they be removed from Britain with very limited rights of appeal.

More than 30,000 asylum-seekers are expected to be affected by the Bill (Ayotte, 1995). The Refugee Council reported that it had seen more than 400 asylum-seekers who faced destitution and homelessness as a result of such decisions. There are no formally collated statistics on the number of Somalis affected by the Bill. However, most of the Somali communities in London know of Somalis who are facing great difficulties. Enshrined in the Somali social system is a social welfare that embraces members in dire needs but most are themselves struggling on the verge of subsistence.

These benefit curbs make no exception for the vulnerable. This means that Somali families with children, sick, elderly or disabled members will not be excepted. Many Somalis are indeed sick or have disabilities as a result of war or long stays in refugee camps and the majority are single mothers with children.

Entitlement to free school meals, uniform grants, free prescriptions and concessionary fees for ESOL and vocational courses are lost under the new regulations. Unaccompanied minors and unaccompanied 16-20 year olds living on severe hardship benefits and the majority of un-accompanied children seeking asylum in the UK come from Somalia.

There is also the matter of the 'Safe' Third Country. As well as bringing in a 'fast track appeals procedure' to asylum applications outside the Geneva Convention, the Bill further reduces the rights of asylum-seekers in 'third country' cases by removing the right of appeal whilst they are still in the UK. The speed of the process under the 'fast track procedure' also makes it difficult for Somali asylum-seekers to get a fair hearing.

These measures are causing particular concern to Somali asylum seekers as they are considered as 'displaced' people by the Home Office and generally travel through another country enroute to the UK. This could lead to a chain of deportation until they are ultimately sent back to Somalia.

The new legislation makes entering or gaining leave to remain in the UK 'by deception' an immigration offence. This will hit the many Somali asylum-seekers who fled Somalia without a valid passport and who generally obtained false documents from transit countries.

According to Clause 8 it is a criminal offence to employ a person who does not have immigration entitlement. A National Insurance (NI) number is considered adequate proof of immigration status but Somalis who do have the right to work are not issued with a NI number until they have employment. This is catch 22, because no employer may accept them without a NI number; and no NI number will be issued until employment is secured. Clause 8 is likely to exacerbate racial discrimination in employment against Somalis.

Impact on Children

It is difficult to predict the potential damage to Somali children of the 1996 Asylum Bill. It will take a while to see how the proposals interact with existing legislation such as the Children Act, the Homeless Persons Act and the National Assistance Act. Much will depend on whether charity organisations and the voluntary sector induce central government to give local authorities grants to cover the extra costs arising from the changes to the benefit system. The children of Somali asylum-seekers face homelessness, education disruption, malnutrition as well as emotional trauma resulting from the uncertainty of their situation. Samiya Aden of the Horn of Africa Somali Women's Organisation (HASWO) in West London expresses the fears of many:

> As a community we have a sense of foreboding that the Bill will only make the current situation of the Somali community much harder, adding to the already deprived social and economic situation.

SETTLEMENT PROBLEMS

Even expatriate workers moving from Somalia to the Arabian Gulf (which have a lot in common) are subject to stress but settling in a Western country is more difficult still. The linguistic and social demands for survival and integration often prove too daunting. A Somali background seems to be more liability than asset. Racial hostility within the host culture isolates Somalis to the fringes of society and they experience a wide gap between reality and expectations. The circumstances which have led to their flight from persecution and torture exacerbate their emotional and psychological stress.

The British climate and social patterns seem to impose an indoor life-style, restricted in space and frequency of social interaction. The high unemployment level – 60-90% amongst adult Somali men – also limits their outdoor activities. The indoor life-style contrasts with the outdoor sociability in Somalia, where women enjoyed an active social life; where children were free to play without any worries for their safety. The limited social interactions and restricted outdoor activity have proved detrimental to health, particularly for women and the elderly restricted to the house by custom, concern or necessity. There is a high incidence of 'muscle and bone rust' accompanied by stress and depression. There have been recent cases of mental illness and instances of suicide, which is totally alien to the Somali culture. Dr Dihod (1996) sees this as a result of cultural shock exacerbated by traumatic experiences in Somalia.

Somalis no longer live in their extended families – the norm at home. Many find the move from traditional extended families to nuclear independence sudden and threatening. At this time of acute stress, family support is cut off. Family separation is also taking its toll. It is quite common for Somali families to arrive in stages. Usually, a mother and her school-age children arrive first and send for the father once asylum status is formalised. This may be a matter of months or years. Such families may feel isolated and long for the familiarity of home. Family reunion after years of separation, often under stressful circumstances, can be difficult as they adjust to each other as 'strangers' in an unfamiliar setting.

As a result of family dispersion, lone parenthood has become wide-spread. Despite prejudice and social stigma and the physical and emotional strain of raising children alone in a difficult environment, many single parents are pragmatic and resourceful. However, another repercussion of family separation is that a relatively large number of Somali children are looked after by older siblings, often scarcely past school age, some of whom can barely cope.

There are an estimated 200 unaccompanied Somali children in Britain. Precise figures are difficult to establish as some unaccompanied Somali children might attach themselves temporarily to a family while passing through immigration or might claim to be older than they really are. Some of these children, aged 17 or under, are either living alone or being looked after by older siblings. Others are in children's homes run by local councils. Lack of parental care and guidance have already taken their toll on these minors, to judge from the reports of incidence of referrals for emotional and behavioural difficulties. Since 1994, children seeking asylum in the UK have come predominantly from Somalia.

The present employment situation in the country can cause changes in the traditional hierarchical structure of the family. The father may be unable to find work and, in his own eyes, will have lost his central position as the head of the family. Loss of the extensive social circle can put a strain on marriages. The rate of separation and divorce within the Somali community is rising. The absence of the traditional arbitration system and the liberal attitudes to marriage in Britain combine to speed up the polarisation. The increasing anxiety about family relationships could have a long-term effect on children, undermining their security and self-esteem and having far reaching implications for their education.

Many Somali parents, particularly mothers who were denied any chance of formal education in their home country, have little proficiency in English and often rely on their children to act as family negotiators and go-betweens. Although this seems convenient and keeps matters confidential, many parents are uneasy about the situation because of the strain on the traditional parent/child relationship. Some youths have part-time jobs at weekends and new responsibilities lead children to claim rights, privileges and independence at ages that would be unthinkable in Somalia itself. (see Coelho, 1994). Parents seem to have lost status and authority while children tend to experience loss of identity and possibly of childhood, taking on responsibility they feel unready to shoulder (cf.Warner, 1992), which can lead to disillusionment, confusion and resentment in the family.

This new nuclear family structure can force children to shoulder serious responsibilities at too early an age – a boy of 14, for example, becoming a surrogate father – and this also has implications for their education.

CULTURE CONFLICT

The liberal, independent-minded culture of the West contrasts with the traditional cohesive sense of belonging that enfolds all generations of the Somali family. Traditional family unity is being undermined and inter-generational frictions are emerging.

Some parents react with fear and suspicion to signs that their children are growing out of their control and are being attracted to aspects of the new culture which they find disturbing (Hassan, 1996). The generations polarise as parents attempt to control exposure and guide their children strictly along Somali cultural values. Any apparent deviation from the norm may incur parental anger and reprimands for even their style of dress. Being a Somali is practically synonymous with being a Muslim and most parents expect their children to dress modestly.

It can be difficult and sometimes confusing for Somali children to resolve the cultural conflicts between home and school. The inherent difficulty may be moderated by the parents' desire that their children fit in at school. Parents generally impress upon their children that while at school they should do what is expected of them; while at home they have to abide by the customs and family norms. In this way, Somali children learn to switch back and forth between the two cultural frames of reference and this – if maintained in equilibrium – can impact positively on their self-esteem and by extension on their school performance.

THE 'REFUGEE' MENTALITY

Somalis generally tend to perceive their settlement in the UK in temporary terms. The older generation, and particularly women, generally express emotional orientation towards their country and are often absorbed by events at home. Although Somalis talk about current events in Britain, it is from social habit rather than a keen interest in the affairs of the host society. Moreover, they rarely establish social relations with members of the mainstream community, due to linguistic and cultural barriers and of course, racism. So for most Somalis, contact with the local people is very limited, as is their knowledge about British life and customs.

Their main leisure pursuit is informal social visits to the homes of relatives and friends. Men usually spend their time in qat chewing sessions. Wedding receptions, Eid festivities and occasional Somali concerts offer one-off social events.

The resurgence of clan consciousness, partly due to the political polarisation at home, creates further factions, thus effectively inhibiting a community spirit or a united front for a fairer share of community grants. External factors, most notably racism and racial prejudice, add to social and economic deprivation. In a nutshell, it is a community in a state of flux: unsettled, neglected and fragmented in attitude and orientation.

QAT: OLD HABITS DIE HARD

The resilience of the Somali family is further tested by the social consumption of qat (catha edulis), green leaves imported fresh in bundles, mainly from Kenya and from Ethiopia and Yemen. Qat is not physically addictive but can induce psychological dependence. Not everyone gets much effect from chewing qat – most common is an initial sense of well-being but regular use can cause a range of effects, from mood swings to psychotic disorders. People who try to quit may suffer withdrawal symptoms.

Somalis are not new to qat; it is rather an old habit that has found a new lease of life in the uncompromisingly harsh experience in the UK. Qat consumption has long been a highly contentious social issue among the Somali community both in the home country and outside. Religious opinions split along traditionalist and liberal lines: the former condemning it and the latter condoning it. Generally, qat chewing is an urban phenomenon but more of the rural population are taking to it. Today many young people in their early teens are using qat but it is still a predominantly male activity, although less exclusively so.

In the UK, the habit, more common with the new arrivals, is often condemned by the more traditional older generation and the 'old-timers', who view it as wasteful indulgence. Proponents, on the other hand, see it as a cohesive social factor and argue that banning it would only alienate an already disenfranchised and polarised community and would probably encourage alcohol consumption and illicit drug use (see Ahmed, 1996, for details). A bunch of qat will cost between £2-£5. In a session, which can last 2-8 hours, an individual will chew an average of two bunches, a serious chewer up to four. A daily chewing session for an 'addict' Somali is not uncommon. Add this to 20 cigarettes plus optional beverages and the costs mount to over £20 per week. Given that over 90% of Somalis are unemployed, this is a big dent on Income Support. Women, who resist qat, resent such self-indulgence at the expense of the family budget. Some men try to cut down but qat is a source of marital tension and this has real implications for the welfare and general development of the children.

The Somali community in London (a microcosm of the Somali community in the UK) is deprived and socially disadvantaged. To sum up, the community suffes from

• an exceptionally high unemployment rate – between 60 to 90% – due to language barriers, racism, lack of marketable skills, lack of knowledge of employment opportunities and of trends in the economy and labour markets, and their limited opportunities for training, etc. (Mohamed and Kahin, 1996).

• a high illiteracy rate of over 35%

• linguistic and cultural barriers due to their lack of English

• housing problems, including homelessness, over-crowded accommodation. Somali refugees spend considerable time in temporary accommodation and are then mostly placed in run-down properties or unpopular high density estates on a permanent basis

• lack of proper community facilities to provide a programme of social and cultural activities, including supplementary classes

• low literacy rate and limited education and training opportunities work against Somalis competing for better prospects

• single parent families, generally headed by women, face additional strains

• racism and racial hostility has not only undermined the community's confidence about acceptance into society but has also inculcated a sense of rejection and exclusion – which further undermines their chances to develop their potential

• The generation gap adds to some children's crisis of identity

• Somalis are generally disenfranchised, having little or no electoral power or access to a political lobby.

Practically all Somali families are on Income Support and their children receive free school meals – classic indicators of their poor economic situation!

Chapter 4

LANGUAGE

Bilingualism is the common language experience of most of the world's population. Rather than constituting a learning difficulty, bilingualism allows for extending cultural and social expression.

Yet, with the exception Welsh and of high status European languages, the languages spoken by significant numbers of bilingual children are generally ignored and devalued in British schools. 'Community languages' becomes a euphemism for institutional disdain and neglect. The teaching of them is at best patchy and not part of the school curriculum. Institutional policy appears to marginalise minority languages and maintain the absolute use of English. The National Curriculum makes scant reference to the language needs of bilingual children. The Cox Report, *Bilingual Children*, refers to bilingual teaching support only as a transitional provision, and is not aimed at supporting the child's bilingualism:

> Where a bilingual pupil needs extra help ... there may be a need for bilingual teaching support ... until such time as they are competent in English (Cox, 1989: 10.10)

Somali, like many other community languages, is wholly disregarded. It would assume only instrumental value, giving way to the eventual supremacy of English. In practice, however, subtractive bilingualism is the case: Somali is not developed and is gradually replaced by English.

There appears to be general paranoia among monolingual teachers and pupils when Somali children code-switch to Somali – a desirable strategy in bilingual communication. Their attitude can affect Somali children, leading them to believe that Somali is linguistically deficient and culturally inappropriate.

The dynamic interplay between the institutional policy, the negative attitude and the misplaced assumptions is potentially detrimental to the social and psychological well-being of Somali children and needs urgent correction. Current research findings indicate the benefits of full bilingual development and the creative interplay between languages (Cummins and Swain 1986; Skutnubb-Kangas, 1988; Fitzpatrick, 1987; Hamers and Blanc,1989; Baker, 1995).

The use of their first language is crucial for both linguistic and literacy development; particularly for children who speak little or no English but are fairly literate in Somali. Mother tongue teaching should therefore be provided for Somali children within school. The real aim should be towards developing the children's bilingualism rather than making a quick transition to English. However, few schools or LEAs show commitment to such provision and there is no political commitment so Somali language learning is condemned to the periphery of supplementary classes. There is a great need for centrally funded and high status programmes to support mother tongue teaching.

In the meantime, schools should understand mother tongue needs and encourage children to use Somali as a complementary aid in education. They should also make some efforts to facilitate the study of Somali to examination level. Such qualifications can be put to use if the family aspire to return to Somalia and the pupils would experience pride in themselves and their culture. Monolingual peers would recognise the unique linguistic skills Somali children possess and this might well enhance their social standing within the class.

A number of boroughs in London, such as Hounslow, Tower Hamlets, Ealing and Harrow, incorporate mother tongues into their education strategies. It is important that others should follow suit. Equally, Somali parents should encourage the use of Somali in tandem with English to increase their chance of the children becoming functionally bilingual, thus extending their career and life options. Mother tongue is vital not only as a main medium of connection with family and community but also as a major part of the child's cultural and ethnic identity.

THE SOMALI LANGUAGE

The official language, Somali belongs to the Cushitic branch of the Afroasiatic family and is related to the languages spoken by the Oromo and Afar in Ethiopia and Djibouti. It has several dialects and regional accents. The dialects are not always mutually intelligible, although nearly all Somalis understand the northern dialect group, which form the basis for Standard Somali (for dialect geography, see Lamberti, 1986). Written Somali shows considerable fluctuation as codification is still in process.

ORAL LITERATURE

The Somali people have an extensive and rich oral literature of stories, proverbs and alliterative poetry of various genres. Apart from their folklore interest, these are often of intrinsically high artistic value and portray a vivid picture of the Somali way of life.

The most important genre amongst the Somali literary tradition is oral poetry. Somalis are known as a nation of poets (see e.g. Hunter, 1880; Burton, 1885; Lawrence, 1954; Andrzejewski, 1963; Lewis, 1964; Johnson, 1972). Poetry is a traditional entertainment which seems to pervade all aspects of life and society. This poetry, known as *maanso* or classical verse, is structurally complex and sophisticated. The demands of the prosody and the cultivated taste of the audiences make the composition of poetry a major intellectual and artistic task (see Andrzejewski, 1963). Somali poetry is alliterative and its rules require the poet to use at least one word beginning with same consonant or with a vowel sound in each line throughout a poem.

Of the several poetic genres, *gabay* is by far the most popular and highly regarded, and earns poets national acclaim and prestige. Although there is no definite restriction on the range of its subject matter, the *gabay* generally deals with serious themes, commenting on public affairs at community or national level and often influencing public opinion (see Lewis, 1961). The Somali Dervish leader, Sayid Mohamed Abdallah Hassan, known by the British as the 'Mad Mullah' effectively used *gabay* to mould public opinion in his nationalist campaign against the British early in this century (see Samater, 1982).

Work and folk dance songs, although entertaining and interesting, are regarded as prosaic and do not merit literary attention. Words are simple and often lack the imagery and subtle distinction found in *gabay.* Modern song poetry, *hees*, despite initial negative publicity, has now acquired fabulous national currency, particularly among the younger generation, supplanting the traditional revered genres in urban and some rural areas (see Johnson, 1974). The modern *hees* is often topical but, like its Western counterparts, of an ephemeral nature, except for some *Qarami* – classical songs – and a few singles by some favourite singers.

Geeraar, a traditional sombre form of poetry, traditionally recited on horseback, and dealing with war and conflict, has lost its popular appeal. *Baraanbur*, exclusively in the domain of female poets, and of equal literary merit, attracts fewer audiences, with only occasional social and cultural events. *Baraanbur* is often accompanied by hand-clapping, drumming or chorus and has a lighter touch than *gabay*.

Only in the early 1940s did theatre emerge as a popular form of entertainment in major cities and towns. Somali plays, *riwaayad*, are inherently an oral art. Actors learn their roles from the playwright without any script. The playwrights, highly talented poets, draw from the rich and varied poetic genres for the most important parts of the dialogue and songs of the play, combining them with impressive style, forceful imagery (at times with esoteric allusions) and captivating effect. The songs are sung to the accompaniment of modern orchestral music that appeals to the younger generation.

The pervasive influence of the transistor and tape-recorder is under-mining the importance of traditional oral literature. On the other hand, techno-oral literature has greatly extended the accessibility of Somali oral culture.

LITERACY

In spite of this great oral tradition, Somali long remained an oral language, with no agreed script. After independence, the new republic found itself with three languages: English, dominant in the north; Italian in the south; and Arabic, shared by both due to the Islamic influence. A suitable script had to agreed – the main contenders were the Osmani script (with characters reminiscent of Amharic), a modi-fied Roman script and a modified Arabic script. The Roman script was preferable for economic and practical reasons. However, public opinion remained divided and only orthographic chaos came out of research projects. There seemed to be a strong deeply historical predilection for using Arabic for formal correspondence and Somali for speech only (Andrzejewski, 1963).

In 1972, Siad Barre adopted the Roman script for the Somali language and it was declared the sole official language for the state, bureaucracy and (in stages) the school system. Concerted urban literacy campaigns ensued, initially directed at government officials. Literacy classes followed, and many people with little or no formal education achieved high literacy levels in Arabic, Italian or English – including women.

By 1974, acceptable standards of urban literacy had been attained and the government decided to take the benefits of the new script to rural areas. A task force of 25,000 students and older school children made their way into the countryside to teach the new alphabet. The motto of the campaign was: 'If you know, teach. If you don't, learn'. The idea was also that young urbanites learn more of the nomadic way of life and the traditions of their country. Sixty percent of the rural population passed the first literacy exam but this has not been sustained (Adam, 1983).

The introduction of Somali into schools as a medium of instruction and literacy campaigns encouraged rapid growth of written literature. By early 1973, news stories and literary writing became a regular feature in the daily *October Star*. School text books and adult literacy primers were prepared by the Ministry of Education. The Somali Academy of Science and Culture was established and published literary works, scholarly dictionaries, social science and history books, also translations of works by foreign authors in varied disciplines. As a consequence, vocabulary in various semantic areas expanded, with new words coined from existing Somali words by compounding or semantic shift and many borrowed words, particularly from Arabic. However, literacy figures for both adults and children are extremely low: the figures indicate less than 25 percent literacy for adults. Literacy is another casualty of the political turmoil and civil unrest and the lack of resources.

Although Somali uses the Roman alphabet, it follows Arabic ordering. Certain letters in Somali indicate entirely different sounds from Arabic. These letters may cause confusion for older children literate in Somali and may result in phonological interference (see below for details).

FACT FILE

- OFFICIAL LANGUAGE: Somali, a Cushitic language.

- SCRIPT: Roman with Arabic ordering

- OTHER LANGUAGES: Arabic, English and Italian.

- LITERACY LEVEL: about 24%

PROBLEMS AREAS IN ENGLISH FOR SOMALI SPEAKERS

In a typical class bilingual children come from different cultural and linguistic backgrounds and difficulties arising from the differences between the children's first language and English have little common ground. However, a knowledge of some of the basic difference in grammar and phonetics can help teachers when they work in withdrawal sessions or individual tuition involving Somali children.

Cummins (1984) and others stress the creative interplay of languages and point out that despite the apparent difference in surface features between, say, Somali and English, there is an underlying proficiency common across languages upon which teachers can build. Somali children who are literate in Somali and/or Arabic have already developed a range of skills and knowledge, some of which are transferable.

This chapter is not based wholly on a contrastive analysis (CA) approach but is used as one means to contribute towards an overall and successful teaching of English to Somali children. Certain errors made by Somali learners of English can be traced to L1 influence, while others are attributable to over-generalisation, simplification or communication-based errors.

THE LANGUAGES NEEDS OF SOMALI CHILDREN

Many Somali children are new to the British education system. Some are literate in Somali and/or Arabic but many more are either non-literate or semi-literate with little previous formal schooling, due to the war. Nearly all receive specialist support of some kind at school. Their needs are more or less the same as other bilingual First/Second Stage* Learners of similar background. However, there is a host of underlying factors (embedded in the Somali background and status within the new country) that seem to undermine the efficacy of any specialist provision.

Bilingual is a term applied to someone developing competence in more than one language (for example in Somali and English). The term does not indicate the competence with which any of the languages is spoken.

The children who are literate in Somali and/or Arabic range from First to Third EAL Stage Learners*. First Stage Learner is applied to bilingual pupils who can take part in classroom activities using first language but need support in English. At secondary level, these pupils need to develop oral/written skills in English and also study skills so that they can work towards examination courses.

The children who are non-literate in Somali or Arabic or are semi-literate, having had some or erratic schooling in Somalia can at best hold a pen properly and form their letters. They are Beginners: that is, having little or no knowledge of English. A new arrival with little or no previous formal schooling will be a total beginner. At secondary level, these pupils need initial intensive EAL/literacy provision to acquire basic skills necessary for participation within the mainstream. They also need to learn about schooling and to develop personal and social skills for integration. Follow-up in-class support is essential.

Pupils with fairly developed oral English but limited literacy are classed as Second Stage Learners. They can take part in most learning activities, but needs considerable support with written English.

All these pupils will have language and literacy problems. They also face social and cultural barriers, finding themselves socially in limbo and facing a new environment that may not accommodate their religious needs. They may well encounter racism and low teacher expectations, and have to adjust to a learning style very different from the formal classrooms of Somalia.

For their part, the teachers are likely to have very little information about the children's cultural/linguistic background, family situation or social concerns. Section 11 funding, although now open to all pupils may still be limited, so restricting the options for specialist provision, such as withdrawal. Specialist resource materials and bilingual materials will seldom be adequate.

Somali pupils may be poorly motivated and have poor attendance. Their learning strategies are inappropriate, as they are familar only with rote learning and not with group or collaborative learning.

Parental support may be of little help. Many Somali parents do not attend parents evenings or school meetings and few of them help their children with homework. Some will occasionally keep children out of school, to help with interpreting, child-minding and help in the home.

As well as these general difficulties faced by Somali children, their language creates specific problems for acquiring a command of English. An understanding of some of the characteristics of Somali will help teachers optimally to support their learning.

The Somali Language

Unlike English, the writing of the Somali language is phonemically regular, so literate Somalis expect a regular relationship between sounds and letters, and teachers need to contrast this regularity with the seemingly chaotic English sound system.

There are 21 consonants, 10 vowels and 5 diphthongs in the Common Somali dialect.

A major difference between Somali and English **consonants** is that certain basic sounds have non-emphatic or no counterparts in English. They are fundamentally different in terms of phonetic nature. These are given below with a brief description to show difference in realisation and articulation:

Consonant	Example	Phonetic Description
1. x	*xayn* – group	voiceless pharyngeal fricative
2. kh	*khad* – ink	voiceless velar or uvular fricative
3. dh	*dhar* – clothes	voiced post-alveolar plosive or retroflex
4. c	*cun* – eat	voiced pharyngeal fricative
5. q	*qalin* – pen	uvular plosive
6. hamsa (')	*gu'*- spring	glottal stop

The Somali language has five short and five long vowels. There are relationships between the short and long vowels in Somali, as illustrated by the following words:

bar (teach) and *baar* (tip)

in (part) and *iin* (defect)

rug (base) and *ruug* (knee)

In other cases, the relationship is complex, marked with shifting back or front articulation of the long vowels.

The following diphthongs occur in Somali:

- *ay* – pronounced /ai/ as in *shay* – thing
- *ey* – pronounced /ei/ as in *meyd* – corpse
- *oy* – pronounced /oi/ as in *hoy* – home
- *aw* – pronounced /au/ as in *hawl* – work
- *ow* – pronounced /ou/ as in *garow* – sorghum

  ey and *ay* are generally interchangeable.

/b, d, f, g, k, l, m, n, r, s, ʃ, j, w/ are equivalent, but there may be difficulties:

- /b/ and /p/ may be confused, /b/ being used for both
- /f/ and /v/ may be confused, /f/ being used for both.
- /θ/ and /ð/ do not occur in Somali and are replaced by /t/ and /d/.

However, /θ/ occurs in classical Arabic and Somali speakers with some knowledge of Arabic may not find this sound difficult.

- /tʃ / and /dʃ / may be confused. The Somali /dʃ/ is sometimes voiced and other times voiceless. The voice and lack of it is arbitrarily optional, but does not create any semantic confusion. Somali children may, therefore, transfer this phonological trait to English and tend to confuse /tʃ/ and/dʃ/ sounds. Extra work may be needed to help them distinguish between the two sounds.
- /ŋ/ occurs only in the sequence /nk/ or /ng/ and it is often replaced by /g/.
- /s/ and /z/ are confused, /s/ being used for both; but /z/ may occur in some borrowed words of Arabic origin.

- /l/ is always clear in Somali, even germinate /l/ is almost always

- /r/ in Somali is usually a weak, voiced, alveolar roll.

- /3/ does not occur in Somali and is often replaced by /ʃ /

Auditory difficulties may affect the Somali child in identifying and distinguishing between the above pairs of sounds, requiring extra work on specific sound distinction linked with pronunciation.

Certain letters in Somali are used to indicate entirely different sounds from English:

- x is a voiceless pharyngeal fricative – close to a strong breathy 'h'.

- kh is a voiceless velar or uvular fricative – closer to 'k' with a fricative articulation

- c is a voiced pharyngeal fricative – closer to 'a' with a pharyngeal articulation and voice.

- q is a voiced uvular plosive – closer to 'k' with voice.

- dh is a voiced post-alveolar plosive – closer to 'd'

These letters may cause confusion and at times phonological inter-ference.

Another pronunciation difficulty is that different consonants in English are pronounced the same:

- ch, ci, s, sh, si, ss, ti are pronounced as 'sh' as in: **ch**ute, so**ci**al, **s**ugar, **sh**ampo, pen**si**on, pre**ss**ure, na**ti**on.

- 's' may be pronounced differently as in: **s**at, **s**ure, ea**s**y.

It is therefore important for teachers to use letter names to explain, particularly for older children, the symbolic relationship between the 26 letters of the English alphabet and the 44 phonemes.

Somali has only pure vowels: five short and five long vowels and only five diphthong sounds. The likely difficulties are:

- /e/ and /i/ are confused /e/ being more likely to be replaced by /i/, particularly in initial position. Both sounds are used in Somali; but /e/ occurs in limited frequency in initial and medial positions.

- /ae/ and /a:/ are confused. The two sounds are not entirely independent and may be interchanged in English.

Long vowels in Somali are not usually long enough to approximate the English long vowel sounds. Special attention must be given to lengthen the long vowels.

- /e:/ is replaced by a long /e/ type or /e/ followed by a Somali /r/.

Centring vowel and diphthong sounds usually cause difficulties:

- /ʊə/ is a difficult sound to produce for Somali learners. They often tend to replace the diphthong with a pure vowel sound /o/.

- /i ə, ə, əʊ / also pose great problems and are replaced by nearest vowel in Somali /e, i , j/ + Somali /r/.

- Inconsistent English orthography will also create some problems, e.g. 'oo' in shoot , foot, door and blood.

- The consonant letters 'r' can combine with vowels to form vowel digraphs; example: farm, herd, girl, short, hurt, etc. The resulting vowel sounds are closer to the Somali long vowels, though they have no orthographic representation in common.

Therefore, if Somali children, in particular older ones with some literacy in mother tongue, were to identify, pronounce and use these vowel digraphs correctly and build on their sight vocabulary at an early stage, they need to learn that the consonant 'r' combines with vowels to symbolise phonemes similar to some of the long Somali vowels.

- Somali has a syllabic structure with single consonants and no clusters. The Somali learner of English is, therefore, inclined to insert a short vowel sound either initially or between adjacent clusters. So for example: film will be pronounced as /filim/ and speed as /ispi:d/.

The phonemes /t/, /k/ and /m/ never occur at the end of a syllable in Somali except in a few words of Arabic origin. Thus, if a word that incorporates one of these sounds is used and occurs at the end of a syllable, it will change to /d/, /g/ and /n/ respectively.

Final clusters which involve these sounds pose difficulties in pronunciation for the Somali child. However, certain final clusters are important, particularly those with morphological significance:

• consonant + /s/	present simple	She sits
• consonant + /z/		She reads
• consonant + /s/	plural/possessive	books, cat's
• consonant + /z/		David's son
• consonant + /t/	past simple/particeple	walked
• consonant + /d/		informed

Somali children may pronounce these words with a vowel insertion between the final consonants. They also tend to voice the /t/ and /k/ sounds at the final clusters.

Stress and intonation

Stress refers to the amount of energy with which a syllable is spoken, whereas intonation is the sound pattern of phrases and sentences. In Somali, stress-tone operates at word level and is determined by the placement of an accent on certain vowels (Orwin, 1995), for example:

– *árday* – pupil – *ardáy* – pupils

– *Soómaali* – a Somali – *Soomaáli* – Somalis

As such, Somali shares similarities with English in relation to word stress; but there the similarities end. Apart from a handful of words, each syllable in Somali has approximately the same length and the same stress and no grouping of syllables into rhythm units as in English. So the English concept of accentuation is totally new. It is therefore important that the Somali speaker should learn the stress pattern of a new word. It is more important to get word stress right than intonation, particularly as monosyllables account for more than 80% in ordinary connected speech (Gimson, 1980).

Somali learners may find it difficult to perceive that certain very common words, e.g. *and, at, can, for*, have two pronunciations – a weak and strong one. They tend to pronounce 'for' in the following question and answer with equal stress: What are you looking *for*? I'm looking *for* my pen.

Grammar

Somali learners of English are likely to display errors which result from applying syntactical rules of L1 to English. The greater the difference between the syntactical forms and patterns between Somali and English, the greater the learning problem and the potential area of interference. Some of these structural errors could simply be communication-based reflecting learner strategies.

Somali is a free word-order language, though the preferred order is probably: subject-object-verb. This remarkable flexibility is often dictated by various syntactic and semantic factors. So in one statement, for example, the word order can be:

> *Axmed tufaaxii wuu cunayaa.* (basic word order is subject-object-verb SOV) Ahmed is _eating_ the apple) or it can be *Axmed wuu cunayaa tufaaxii* (SVO) *Tufaaxii wuu cunayaa Axmed* (OVS) *Wuu cunayaa tufaaxii Axmed* (VOS).

The change in the word order does not signal any major semantic shift or confusion, though the order of constituents is semantically or pragmatically significant and the same rule applies to other kinds of sentences, for example, in a negative sentence *Ma jecli midabkaas* or *Midabkaas ma jecli.* (I don't like that _colour_) or in questions: *Mee furahaygii? Furahaygii mee?* (Where is my key?). *Miyuu Axmed cunnay qadadiisii?* or *Axmed miyuu cunnay qadadiisii?* or *Qadadiisii miyuu Axmed cunnay?* (Did Ahmed eat his lunch?). The same applies to the imperative: *Ha taaban waxba* or *Waxba ha taaban.* (Don't touch anything).

Somali learners of English may tend to transfer such variable word order in Somali to English and make mistakes in relation to English sentence patterns and will need structured practice of basic word order and sentence patterns in English.

The use of **adjectives** is another problem area. Somali adjectives invariably come after the noun, for example: *Shaadh cas.* (A red shirt). *Guri weyn.* (A big house).

Comparative/superlative, in particular, operate in Somali in different syntactical formation – through the use of an auxiliary noun and prepositions.

Somali uses a wide range of **tenses**. The perfect tense, however, is not used and Somali learners of English often tend to replace it with the simple past or assign the wrong tense. For example: I studied English for three years. I have just ran a mile.

They need practice to learn that the present perfect and simple past tenses do not have the same uses. It will take some time before they internalise the difference between them and use them correctly.

Prepositions almost always pose difficulties for the bilingual learner of English irrespective of linguistic background. Even monolingual children find prepositions a problem. In Somali, there are four locative prepositions: *ka, ku. la* and *u*; and four deictic prepositions: *soo, sii, wada* and *kala*. Somali prepositions occur with each other, with pronouns, with negatives and with conjunctives. Some verbs do not require any preposition: it is built into the word – *tag* – 'go away' or 'go to'. Unlike in English, prepositions come before the verb. There are also other prepositions of place in frequent use; but they come after the noun or pronoun to relate it grammatically or semantically to another constituent of the sentence. For example: *waddada dhinaceeda* (along the road), *miiska dushiisa* (on the desk).

Moreover, the use of prepositions in Somali is not as extensive or semantically charged as in English. The most common errors that result are leaving out the preposition: 'I'll see you Sunday'. Wrong use of preposition: 'I was born on March'. Inserting a unnecessary preposition: 'My dad is coming to home soon'.

Subject/verb agreement is also problematic, when the auxiliary or main verb ends with -s, -es, or -is. Somali learners tend to leave out these morphemes for example: 'Mummy come home late' or 'She don't like ice-cream'. Nouns ending in 's' which are in fact singular: 'Bad news travel fast'. Plural subject with singular verb: 'Asha and Ali has just left'.

Somali has a wide range of **pronouns** for all cases except the reflexive. Somali pronouns function basically the same as their English counterparts; however, the inherent linguistic difference of the two languages may result in confusion. Common mistakes are confusing the subjective/objectives cases: 'Me hit him first' or 'He just hit she for no reason'. Failing to agree pronoun with verb: 'She don't finish her homework' or placing a pronoun immediately after the subject: 'My mum she looks after me'.

Somali uses a choice of definite **articles** dictated by gender and noun ending and they invariably come after the noun. There is no indefinite article before the noun – the absence of it marks the indefinite nature of the noun. The common errors that may result are: confusion of 'a' and 'an' using the letters instead of the vowel sounds as guide: 'an university, a honourable man' or using articles incorrectly: 'The sugar is bad for your teeth'. Or articles are omitted: 'Give me rubber'; 'The earth goes round sun'. NB Pronunciation of 'the' before a vowel or consonant sound is a potential difficulty.

Direct questions can present difficulties in their structural formation, in particular question tags and in intonation. 'Who' and 'which' may be confused: 'Which is your English teacher?' or subject-auxiliary inverted: 'What time it is now?'

In question tags, auxiliaries are often wrongly used in 'You saw, haven't you?'; 'He has left, didn't he?' And negative/positive elements may be misplaced: 'He scored a goal, did he?'; 'He can't read, can't he?'

Spelling

English spelling is inconsistent. Certain sounds are regularly written in more than one way. Often there are rules that show which spelling to use but not always. A Somali child, used to a phonetically regular language, where the sound/k/, for example, is always spelt 'k', discovers that the English /k/ sound can be spelt: c, cc, ch, ck, k, q, qu and que. Somali has no silent letters at all so these, too, are a problem.

English has a wide range of variants and many words which defy phonic rule, for example: head, fear, heal. These basic words cause problems in both pronunciation and spelling for Somali learners of English.

Doubling the consonant also precipitates spelling mistakes. However, comparison can be made with Somali here.

In English, if a word ends in a single vowel+ a single consonant, the consonant is doubled before adding the morphological endings-er,-est, -ed, -ing, -y (see chart page 62).

In Somali, if a word ends in a single vowel+ the consonants: b, d, r, g, l, m, and n, maybe doubled before adding the morphological endings: -ay, -o, -aal, -aan.

English

Single consonant	example	
b	rub	rubbed
d	bid	bidder
r	stir	stirring
g	big	biggest
l	travel	travelling
m	hum	hummed
n	fun	funny
p	tap	tapping
t	sit	sitting

Somali

Single consonant	example	
b	*cab* (drink)	*cabbay* (drank)
d	*rid* (shoot)	*riddo* (shooting)
r	*far* (finger)	*farriin* (message)
g	*rog* (turn over)	*roggal* (turning)
l	*dha* (give birth)	*dhallaan* (children)
m	-	*lammaan* (couple)
n	*fan* (art)	*fannaan* (artist)

Note: *The same consonants double both in English and Somali, taking into account that in Somali the same sound represents the /b/ and /p/ phonemes and the Somali phoneme/t/ never occurs in the final position.*

Style and Register

Language and culture are intertwined and words often express particular attitudes or particular contexts. Somali children are not fully socialised with mainstream culture and may find it difficult to grasp the fine socio-linguistic features appropriate for different registers. Bilingual children of similar background usually experience problems in understanding and using correctly some of the specialised literary features. However, the following may pose particular difficulties to Somali children: idiomatic expressions; figurative usage; polite expressions and slang/taboo words

Somali uses a wide and sophisticated range of idiomatic expressions and figurative usage but they operate on different socio-linguistic parameters to English. Somali speakers find it easy to understand and use the English idioms and figurative expressions which are semantically clear or have similar notions in Somali. On the other hand, culturally embedded and semantically ambiguous ones cause difficulties. For example: As easy as ABC is semantically clear, while as easy as pie is semantically ambiguous. Similarly figurative expressions may be semantically clear, eg. It makes my heart ache... but An ache of despair is semantically ambiguous.

Somali and English differ on polite expressions. There is no equivalent in Somali to 'please'. In Somali relational terms such as brother, uncle, etc. are often employed to introduce or end requests.

There is an equivalent in Somali for 'thank you' but no conventional response. Some individuals may use some paralinguistic feature as a way of response or perhaps say *adaa mudan.*

Words that are considered slang or thought obscene or shocking in the one culture may not carry the same intensity or effect in the other. Moreover, Somali children may fail to detect the subtle connotations of slang and taboo words or may pick them up and inappropriately use them.

Note
* Not all education authorities in the UK use EAL 'stages'. The number of 'stages' also varies, some using up to 6. Moreover, while some authorities use simple assessment procedure, others, like Manchester, use a complex one. Some of the 'stages' are clearly linked to the National Curriculum(NC); others also reflect 'pre' NC levels. The 'stages' referred to here are those used by Hounslow Language Service.

Chapter 5

THE EDUCATIONAL NEEDS OF SOMALI CHILDREN

To help Somali pupils to achieve optimally, teachers will need an understanding of not only the issues that relate specifically to their language but also of certain issues relating to their background, culture and religion.

RELIGION
Somali parents attach great importance to the religious up-bringing of their children. Religious observance and faith is a daily part of their lives.

Religious beliefs and attitudes are modified by membership of educational or other social groups. So values acquired in school can conflict with values learnt at home and in the community. As a consequence, many young Somalis, constantly exposed to the dominant culture through school life, the neighbourhood and the media, tend to take aspects of Islam less seriously than their parents feel they ought to. This is exacerbated by inadequate provision for the religion of Somali children in the maintained sector and the lack of proper public and community facilities for parents to transmit regularly religious behaviour, beliefs and experience to children in the way that parents would do in Somalia.

Schools can nonetheless play an important role in the children's moral and spiritual education, both through their underlying ethos and the formal curriculum. LEAs and schools should be sensitive and well informed about the needs specific to Muslims.

Prayer (*Salat*)

Somali parents are concerned that their children are not generally able to perform their *salat* (prayer) at school. Salat is a major aspect of Muslim faith and a daily obligation to be performed at set times. The timings of the prayer sessions vary according to sunrise and sunset but morning and evening sessions do not normally conflict with the school day. However, noon and afternoon prayers do present difficulties, especially in the winter season.

Somali children often feel their faith is being compromised within the confines of the classroom. They may be constrained by the rigid school timetable or the lack of a suitable washing and praying area. In certain schools, the RE department makes some provision; in others, it is left to the discretion of the EAL department. Schools should make proper provision to allow children to practice their faith. Either the timetable is flexible at midday or children are permitted to withdraw for a short time to respond to their religious duty (see Parker-Jenkins, 1991). Schools should also provide a prayer room and washing facilities for ablution. Friday prayer is very important. Schools with Muslim children should either extend the lunch time break or allow a local imam to lead the prayer on school premises.

Fasting during Ramadan

Ramadan is considered a holy month in which Somalis, along with other observant Muslims, focus on the spiritual dimension and strengthen their faith. Fasting is obligatory, but rigorous observance is not expected until puberty. Fasting goes beyond the mere abstinence from food, drink and sexual activities and involves sincerely refraining from all immoral deeds and thoughts. During Ramadan, the day begins with a pre-dawn meal – *Suhur* – followed by morning prayers and meditations. There will be no breakfast and no food or drinks during the day.

Because of the psychological and spiritual demands that it makes, fasting can never be reduced to a formality. On the practical side, sleeping patterns change with the prescribed eating order and this has implications for schooling. Schools need to understand what Ramadan entails for their pupils.

Some Somali children may wish to fast a little when they are quite young, gradually building up over the years until the point when they can make a complete fast, ideally, at secondary school age. This way, their health is not damaged and they do not put off fasting altogether. However, as the glucose level goes down, children may feel lethargic and find it difficult to concentrate or undertake physically demanding activities. Accordingly schools need to review the school timetable to accommodate the observance of Ramadan so as to reduce demands of PE and sports activities. Assessed tasks, particularly SATs or school exams, should be held in the morning during Ramadan.

To an outsider, fasting may seem to be difficult, uncomfortable or distracting. To Muslims, however, it is a joyful act of worship and supreme spiritual cleansing. Teachers who have little or no knowledge about the importance and nature of fasting may inadvertently interfere by making negative comments or, perhaps well-meaningly, offer a child a drink or try to discourage the fast. Teachers should be informed that Islam stresses that fasting should not harm health: hence, the frail and the sick are exempted and if fasting makes someone sick, it should be abandoned. Ramadan is considered very important among Somalis and even children who neglect their prayer generally keep their fast. They are certainly subject to community (including peer) disapproval if they don't. Fasting means a lot to these children both in terms of personal achievement and a sense of belonging.

As a holy month, it is customary for many Somalis, young and old, to increase their spiritual activities during Ramadan. They pray more, read the Qur'an and contemplate. At school, many more Somali children may perform Salat during lunch time. This means that they will need a larger space than the usual prayer room to be made available. Washing facilities for ablution before prayer will be essential. Arrangements should also be made to enable them to attend the Friday Prayer.

Eid Festivities
Eid-al-Fidri and Eid-al-Adha are important Muslim festivals. They are integral parts of the religion. Somali parents attach much importance to these joyous festivals and treat them as family occasions. Traditionally, festivities for each go on for three days so it is not uncommon for Somali children to miss school. Schools should make the Eid days an authorised absence.

Localised Customs

Muslims in the UK come from Africa, Asia, the Middle East and elsewhere. Though they share the basic principles of Islam, different communities have different interpretations of the religion and some may adopt puritanical observance (for more on this, see Parker-Jenkins, 1995). Even within the Somali community different families tend to interpret the religion differently. There are some areas of concern of which schools need to know regarding the fasting of Somali children.

Some children may refuse to take an afternoon shower for fear it may make their fasting null and void. Fasting pupils generally make special efforts not to lose their temper and to get on well with others. They may even refrain from normal fun and games. Some children may not swallow their own saliva and so spit into tissues or waste paper baskets.

Dietary Needs

Somali parents have expressed concern over the food their children are given at school. Few schools serve halal food in their canteens even though Jewish children have 'kosher' meat and although awareness of the dietary needs of the Muslim and other ethnic minority children appears to be growing.

Collective Acts of Worship

The Education Reform Act (1988) requires all maintained schools to provide daily collective worship on broadly Christian lines. The Education Reform Act gives schools the right to apply, through their local Standing Advisory Committee on Religious Education (SACRE), for alternative worship or withdrawal from collective worship. Any school assembly with a religious content other than Islam can be of concern to Somali parents. School assemblies should be made more relevant and accessible to children from different cultures and creeds and schools with a majority of Muslim children require time and a place allocated for their worship, especially the Friday communal prayer. Somali parents should also be informed of the nature of RE and assemblies and their right to withdraw their children.

CURRICULUM AND LEARNING

While provision for special religious needs will benefit pupils, allowing them to avoid working hard is bad for all concerned. It can lower teacher expectations and allow pupils to become complacent. If they are not challenged they cannot acieve their potential. Somali children who are academic may become frustrated or stifled in a school that fails to challenge them and their misdirected energy could lead to unacceptable behaviour. So while teachers need to be aware of the difficulties faced by the children they should still encourage them to work to the same standard as their peers. Teachers should use their professional judgement to strike the right balance.

Certain Somali children with pronounced learning difficulties who slip through the net and are not referred for specialist help should have their cases reviewed. The needs of Somali children with war injuries or health problems caused by periods spent in refugee camps or exposure to war should not be under-estimated.

EAL Support teaching provides specialist support to pupils with language and literacy needs. However, support is not forthcoming as an integral part of every lesson. When there is no specialist support, Somali pupils (like many other bilingual First/Second Stage Learners) may be left out or occupied with marginal tasks. It is important that ways should be found to adapt the lesson so that all pupils can participate and learn from it.

English has its inherent linguistic and cultural bias and can be unsuitable for assessment. Researchers have indicated the importance of assessing bilingual pupils who have been 'statemented' in their first language (Cummins, 1984; Hall, 1995). Language and literacy problems may be confused with conceptual and learning difficulties (Hall, 1995) especially when assessing Somali children with no previous formal education. A bilingual professional should be included in any multi-discipline assessment, as is already done in a number of boroughs, such as Hounslow, Harrow and Tower Hamlets. Information about statementing processes should be made accessible to Somali parents and they should be informed of their right to be involved. Too often, decisions are seen to be made by professionals and families are left out of the decisions which will affect the educational future of the children. The schools should make it clear to parents and children that they value the Somali culture and language.

In Somalia, entry to a particular year of education does not necessarily depend on age. Recently arrived Somali children are seriously disadvantaged by the British education system which is 'year-governed', grouping children according to their age. This hinders a flexible response to the many Somali children who need more time to acquire literacy and linguistic skills. Somali parents and teachers may suggest that a child be put down a year because of their low language and literacy levels. LEAs should develop flexible admission and transfer procedures, to accommodate the language and literacy needs of Somali children.

Unlike other relatively well established ethnic minority groups, the Somali community has few support staff in education and other related services. Initial training and recruitment of social workers, liaison officers, education welfare officers and nurses from the community is vital, and the community needs practical help to become self-sufficient by building a strong support network.

Somali parents generally maintain minimal contact with school because of linguistic, cultural and practical constraints. Many find the schools alien and somewhat intimidating. In Somali culture, the role of the teacher is seen as distinct and separate from parenting so they feel their presence might be intrusive and undesired and leave it all to the school. Schools, for their part, often only contact the parents when their children are in trouble. Yet effective home/school relations are vital if children are to get the most from their education. Home/school links must be made more responsive and meaningful and this will happen only when schools are able to identify parental needs, wishes and experience and are willing to respond to them in a spirit of practical partnership (Bastiani, 1989). Liaison between home and school generally tends to relate to problems in school, rather than to the advantages of good channels of communication and working together.

Education is a partnership venture and good home/school links an integral part of good schooling. Teachers responsible for home/school links should be given information about the special needs and concerns of Somali children. Representatives from the Somali community should be encouraged to become school governors, and parents to join parent/teacher associations. This is more likely to be sustained and successful if two or three of the Somali parents join the committee at the same time.

Many schools make an effort to communicate information to Somali parents through newsletters, parents evenings, open days, etc. but if these are only in English, many Somali parents are excluded. To make information widely accessible, a network of bilingual support is needed. Through this network, Somali parents can be helped to understand more about the education system and schools and encouraged to take an active interest in the education of their children. Relying on a bilingual relative or friend can simply create misunderstanding.

Few Somali parents have any experience of the British education system. In a 1996 survey by Somalink, almost half of the educated respondents replying said that they know little about the British education system. It is up to schools to communicate with Somali families about the school's organisation, the curriculum and about parental rights. It is for the school to ensure that information and advice flow in both directions and involve Somali parents in the life of the school.

For their part, parents express certain concerns about their children's schools. They have problems with school meals and fear lest their child is eating food that is not halal. Their concern for modesty and privacy, especially in changing rooms, is not met by facilities for PE and games. Due to an absence or poor network of bilingual support, they and their children lack access to information on careers, school policy, option choices etc. They find schools failing to prevent their children from suffering racial harassment/abuse. They are deeply concerned about their children underachieving at school but feel that they are given little support. They are concerned about their own inability in many instances to be more involved in their children's education, unable to help with homework, to attend school meetings or parents evenings, or to negotiate appropriate option choices with school. The opting-out policy and league tables seem in reality to be hindering rather than helping them exercise their parental choice of school because they are not fully informed about such issues.

SUPPLEMENTARY AND SATURDAY CLASSES
Because schools are failing to provide adequately for Somali children the community needs to establish supplementary classes to enable the children to derive more from their mainstream schooling. The curriculum needs to be expanded to include tuition in maths, science, and English and to clarify mainstream subjects. Somali parents view their

children's prolonged participation in the British education system as undermining their Somali identity, as children increasingly conform to the values and behaviour of the school peer group. They hope that sending them to supplementary classes will counter some of these effects and provide an environment where Somali cultural values can be transmitted to children (Aden, 1995).

While some supplementary schools are well run and enterprising, many of them are beset by organisational and structural problems. Most are run on a voluntary basis by community members who are not trained in school management. Working conditions and facilities are generally poor; classes are large; trained, qualified teachers sparse; and there are scant financial resources to pay teachers and buy equipment.

Mainstream schools can play an active part in helping secure funding and accommodation, both of which are difficult to come by. Community centres can serve not only as a base for supplementary classes and social activities but also for maintaining close ties within the community to preserve its cultural heritage.

COMMUNITY/SCHOOL LINKS

The Somali community remains isolated from mainstream British culture through a combination of social deprivation, linguistic/cultural barriers and racial prejudice. Somali adults usually have very limited social interaction with the British community, children at school often socialise within the Somali peer group, and the older they are the more evident this is. It is especially difficult for Somali children arriving at secondary level to integrate socially, when they speak little or no English, don't know playground games, or the rituals and symbols of peer culture and generally feel overwhelmed by their sudden exposure to an alien culture.

Schools therefore need to take an active role in facilitating the Somali community's participation in and enjoyment of the educational, social and recreational life they offer. For Somali children, school visits and trips and sports activities mean more than routine school functions. Their parents may be reluctant to allow them to take part in extra-curricular activities, possibly because they regard school outings and events as social occasions and do not appreciate their educational value. Moreover, school outings may create cultural and practical problems to do with food and sleeping arrangements as well as security. The issue of money should also not be overlooked, as many families live on Income Support. However, schools can maximise the active participation of their Somali pupils and with consultation and explanation, there is a good chance of obtaining parental consent.

Links with the community should be established and strengthened. Senior school students can be involved more actively in community service through work experience/community placements. A community service co-ordinator can benefit all concerned by ensuring responsive and accessible community/school link procedures.

GENERATION GAP

Somali children carry with them a deep sense of family loyalty and awareness of their cultural heritage. However, the contradictions that inevitably develop between traditional Somali values and the value system of the host community can lead to a culture clash. This tends to be felt most powerfully by teenage Somalis, who may exhibit patterns of behaviour that are regarded as unacceptable to their older relatives. A gulf between them and their parents is virtually inevitable but some tensions may be alleviated by the hierarchy and emotional relationships characteristic to the Somali family.

Nevertheless, subtle but pervasive racial discrimination seems to be taking its toll on Somali children. Not all identify positively with their culture and linguistic background; and many internalise the negative views which the host community generally has of ethnic minority groups, their language and culture. There are even instances of Somali children disowning their community and culture and try to shift their identity – only to meet indifference, if not disdain, from the mainstream community. For these children, the outcome can be a form of identity crisis. Of course, cultural values and attitudes are not fixed or static. The dynamics of the situation in relation to the settlement process often dictates acceptance and adoption of some of the cultural values of the dominant community, until an acceptable compromise is reached.

DUAL SOCIO-CULTURAL SETTINGS

The presence of Somali children in the classroom demands of them behaviour which may be alien to their cultural repertoire. Their posture, gestures and facial expressions may be unfamiliar to their teachers and fail to conform to the norms of acceptable behaviour. Teachers may possibly find difficulty interpreting some of these paralinguistic codes of communication.

For instance, within Somali social etiquette, looking down or turning the eyes indicates deference and respect to an adult. Yet it is often misinterpreted as bad manners or a sign of guilt and can result in sanctions.

To take two other examples: Somali girls come from a cultural background where the seclusion of women and modesty in their dress is the norm and they are expected to be self-effacing. They are generally resistant to physical contact with members of the opposite sex and try to keep their distance in a discreet manner, but may at times become tense. It is a rule among Muslims to honour the right hand above the left. The right hand is used for all honourable purposes and the left for actions which, though necessary, are considered unclean. Somalis customarily do not use the left hand for giving, pointing or shaking hands and a pupil may even refuse to accept something handed to her with the left hand, as she would consider this impolite.

Somali children are being socialised within two cultural settings which can give rise to misunderstandings and to heightened ethnic self-consciousness. Teachers should understand and acknowledge the different cultural values, norms and experience of Somali children in relation to their classroom behaviour.

EXPERIENCE AT SCHOOL

The first experience of school for any child can be daunting, bewildering and at times overtaxing. How much more difficult and stressful for a Somali child with no previous formal education, little or no English and limited experience of urban life to be suddenly exposed to the life of a British school?

Even children with some experience of school in Somalia find the transition confusing and stressful. They are used to a totally different ethos. They are puzzled by the different teacher/pupil relationship, comparatively lax discipline and more relaxed school routine. They may feel lost or insecure in a class where the teacher does not direct or monitor every stage of the lesson. The range and profusion of equipment in the school may seem overwhelming and intimidating.

The Somali tradition of teaching will influence the way some Somali children adapt to school routine, both in general and in their performance in particular curriculum areas. Homework may pose a particular challenge as few will have encountered it back home, so teachers need to develop strategies for helping pupils with their homework. Once taken on board, homework tends to dominate household activities among Somali families on week nights, with many parents helping their children with homework. Even those who lack formal education or facility with English generally set standards and goals for each evening.

Art and Design may cause difficulties for Somali children. Unlike the oral tradition, visual arts are little developed in Somalia. The creation of 'graven images' is discouraged on theological grounds and as result the carving of wooden masks or statues, clay modelling and casting are rarely practised. Somali children may not only lack previous experience of artistic representation but may be unfamiliar with the varieties of visual materials used in the classroom. Some will have artistic talent but it will take them some time to master the basic techniques and skills. It is likely, though, that parental dislike of drawing and painting may stifle a budding talent. Somali parents generally regard certain curriculum areas, such as Art, Music, PE, as non-educational and are not interested in their children excelling in them.

TRAUMATIC EXPERIENCES

Evidence is accumulating that exposure to war and violence have adverse effects on children's emotional and mental health (Punamak, 1987; Kinzie et al, 1989; Baker, 1992; Bonnet, 1993). A relatively large number of Somali children seeking asylum in the UK have lived through traumatic experiences of war and displacement. Although there is no research specifically targeted, mainly due to the chaotic and dangerous environment in Somalia, anecdotal evidence is growing of manifest emotional and behavioural problems among Somali children at school as result of exposure to the war.

Somali refugee children have experienced varying degrees of personal trauma. Some children may have first-hand experience of the brutality of war: witnessing the killing of loved ones and the destruction of their homes. Some may have been abandoned or orphaned and left without emotional or material support. Some children may have been arrested, detained or tortured or, in the case of girls, been subjected to gang rape. Some may have been wounded or suffered severe disablement. Some boys may have become active participants in the war, voluntarily joining or forcibly recruited to fight alongside adults soldiers.

Some children may have trekked for miles across the border to safety; some have spent many years in refugee camps, often in appalling conditions. Some children have been displaced in no-man's land, experiencing shortages of food, water or other necessities. Others have lived with the fear and stress of constant strafing and shelling; while others have no direct experience of the war but may have lived in constant fear for the safety of family members and friends.

The civil war in Somalia has caused suffering in many ways: destruction, displacement and destitution have occurred on a massive scale. The traumatic and emotional effects of war are often the most difficult to gauge, but at times these effects can be much more profound than the physical aftermath. UNICEF (1992) estimate that well over a million people have suffered psychological trauma.

In view of the diversity of experience, one would counsel caution in attempting to formulate a simple checklist of the emotional and social consequences of exposure to war. As well as the varying personal trauma, a range of mitigating factors is likely to influence the impact of war on the child, including family and community support. A general outline of some of the common disorders may, however, shed light on the pervasive effect of war on the behaviour and attitudes of Somali children and so promote early intervention to check any potential deterioration.

In the classroom, traumatised children may manifest the following behaviour:

* difficulty in settling in and concentrating

* lethargy and lack of motivation

* withdrawal and depression

- phobia and anxiety
- preoccupation with death and destruction
- somatic problems: headache, stomach pain, etc.
- reactions of intense anxiety
- aggression or irritability.

On the playground traumatised children can find it difficult to react in a balanced way. Their reaction can be extreme and unpredictable. Boys, in particular, are likely to respond physically to taunts and racial abuse.

Somali children's previous stressful experience is in a dismally large number of instances exacerbated by their exposure to daunting school environments for which they feel inadequately prepared. There is a danger that they are seen as disruptive and naughty or racially stereotyped when in reality they are suffering from post-traumatic stress disorder. A relatively large number of children need counselling of some sort. They require, first, to be listened to in a quiet and relaxing atmosphere. Extreme patience is required during the recovery period which can take months or even years. But few teachers are trained as professional counsellors, so are likely to find any deep personal exchanges painful and overwhelming. Arbitrary measures will be ineffective. Clear policy and procedures should be developed to enable traumatised children to settle down. There are some schools and education authorities who are setting up counselling facilities to respond to the emotional and psychological needs of refugee children (see Klein, 1994). Each school requires a teacher who has counselling skills and speedy referral systems to specialist counsellors for children who are severely traumatised. Counselling should take account of the delicate cultural issues affecting Somali children.

RACISM

Racial prejudice and racism permeate the fabric of our lives and discriminatory practices are affecting Somali children in Britain. The educational system is essentially monocultural and assimilationist-oriented as is evident in curriculum content, assessment methods, school ethos and teacher attitudes in many schools.

Most Somali children are noticeably proud of their cultural identity and physical appearance and this helps them to sustain the high self-esteem which can cushion racial taunts and abuse. This does not, however, make them impervious to the pervasive effects of racism, which has already undermined their cultural and linguistic identity – nor is racist behaviour acceptable. Schools should create an ethos which aims to encourage teachers and pupils to understand, value and respect linguistic and cultural diversity and work towards social justice and cohesion.

INDUCTION PROGRAMMES AND EAL PROVISION

Induction programmes and EAL provision for bilingual children vary from one LEA to another. Some have a team of specialist teachers working on a peripatetic basis; in others children are withdrawn on a part-time basis; in others immediate immersion seems the preferred strategy for full access to the National Curriculum (NC). All these strategies fail to take into account the special instructional needs of Somali children. In order to be appropriate and effective, induction courses need to:

- introduce core NC areas in a friendly (and preferably bilingual) environment and through stages compatible with the children's abilities, knowledge and experiences

- ensure progressive language learning with relevant and meaningful NC content, to provide a substantive basis for language learning

- engage in progressive exposure to mainstream class to ensure smooth transition for the child, and

- provide follow-on in-class support and an additional EAL/literacy component to prevent pupils floundering in the mainstream.

Such provision seems practical and operates in some boroughs. It involves withdrawing Beginners and First Stage learners to an intensive language programme which offers core NC subjects as well as other curriculum areas. These are taught by specialist EAL teachers with some training/knowledge of other subjects in the curriculum. In certain areas of the curriculum such as Physical Education, Information Technology, Personal and Social Education, Arts and Drama, children are catered for in the mainstream.

In this way, Somali children (and other bilinguals) are allowed access to the whole curriculum through progressive exposure which combines both academic achievement and social integration. Some children with no previous education or who are severely traumatised as a result of war and flight are given full withdrawal for some time to adapt to school life and classroom routine as well as acquiring basic language and literacy skills. The children's progress is regularly reviewed every half term. Not only is the individual pupil's language/literacy ability considered but also their social integration and emotional stability, before steps are taken to return a pupil to mainstream.

A teacher should be appointed with special responsibilities for refugee children, to arrange assessment and induction of new arrivals and liaise with relevant services and agencies so as to provide a comprehensive support network. It is important that all schools establish some procedure for new arrivals, starting with a tour of the school building for both parents and pupils to introduce them to the school's organisation, curriculum and ethos. Ideally, Somali parents should receive a welcome booklet in English/Somali that gives basic information about the school's requirements and about their rights for free schools meals, uniform grants and transport fares (see Coelho, 1994). Somali parents also need to understand the education options available to their children and the role they can play in the education of their children.

HOUSING PROBLEMS

The Somali community generally faces unsettling housing problems when they come to Britain, stemming mainly from their immigration status. A relatively large number of the Somali community are asylum seekers and are not offered full refugee status. Asylum seekers are often put in temporary accommodation, where they usually remain for as long as it takes the Home Office to process their application – anything from two to three years.

They are frequently housed in run-down properties and some local authorities increasingly tend to group Somali families in unpopular high density estates and in overcrowded conditions. A typical Somali family of six with additional extended family members would find a three-bedroom house/flat insufficient to meet their accommodation needs.

Such accommodation problems definitely have implications for the education of Somali children. Some families in temporary accommodation move house many times, so the children have to move from one school to another, disrupting their education at a critical time when they need to settle down in school. Such experiences damage their education and the lack of a suitable study area in their overcrowded living conditions (Power et al, 1996) also affects their studies. The Asylum Act (1994) housing amendment, which subjects asylum seekers to temporary accommodation, requires review. And local authorities need to eliminate discriminatory practices in their housing allocation policies and introduce fair distribution systems.

CAREERS EDUCATION AND GUIDANCE

Careers education and guidance significantly affects children's choice of destination on leaving school. Pupils need help to make well-informed educational and training choices and manage the transition from school to adult and working life. Due to inherent linguistic and cultural barriers, Somali girls need particularly sympathetic and sensitive guidance. Certain cultural and practical factors should be taken into account, as well as the subtle and overt barriers that may hinder their progress:

Career Exhibitions: Somali parents may not be informed about the different options available to their children. They need to know about the current trends in the economy and the labour market as well as educational/vocational opportunities. It is therefore imperative to organise accessible career exhibitions, at least on a yearly basis. This could be arranged centrally through the LEA to maximise attendance.

Parental Expectations: education is generally highly valued by Somali refugees and is often seen as providing their only hope for the future, so they have high expectations of their children, expectations that are not always realistic. Careers Education should try to reconcile such aspirations with realistic possibilities that balance parental expectations with their children's inclinations and abilities.

Option Choices: Option choices should go beyond 'choice in theory'. Somali children need to participate in decisions about the courses they follow. Somali children are generally less likely than others to get places on overcrowded courses. It is important that they are given equal access. (see Gillborn, 1990). They are more likely to be recommended for vocational rather than academic subjects. Such recommendations seem to be based on their level of English rather than on academic achievement or potential. Somali children with language problems should have access to interpreting/translation facilities particularly at key decision-making stages – i.e. 13+, 16+ and 17+.

Work Experience is important not only to give a taste of practical skills but, more importantly, as a transition into adult and working life. In organising work experience, it is important to challenge racial stereotypes while at the same time taking into consideration cultural and gender issues.

UNDERACHIEVEMENT

The academic achievements of Somali children are limited both in comparison with their peers and in terms of their potential. A preliminary survey by Somalink in 1996 of 120 pupils at 16 different schools, showed that less than 30% of Somali children entered for GCSE in 1995/6 achieved grades A-C in more than 5 subjects, against the national average of 43.3%. The results were even worse in the inner-city London boroughs of Tower Hamlets and Hackney.

There is also an emerging trend of marked underachievement in literacy, and this greatly concerns Somali parents. A relatively large number of Somali children, from different social and educational backgrounds, tend to achieve marginal literacy levels in English, even those who have already spent up to five years or more in British schools. Many of these children currently receive SEN provision. It is difficult to say how much affective and educational factors contribute to their low literacy levels, and comprehensive research into the root causes of the problem is urgently needed. Some of the factors that appear to contribute to this situation are:

- Language and literacy problems – a relatively large number of Somali children have had little or no formal education before coming to England. Those with previous schooling had their education severely disrupted by political unrest and civil war in Somalia.

- Children who arrive in the UK at age 11 or over with little or no previous schooling, stand little chance of going beyond the acquisition of basic social skills, which do not in themselves facilitate academic learning (Cummins, 1981; Collier, 1989).

- Many Somali families do not currently enjoy stable, settled housing arrangements.

- Functional literacy in the home environment may be limited and there are insufficient effective supplementary classes.

- Because of the social segregation of the Somali community, the children's exposure to English is limited.

- There is a tendency for teachers to label Somali refugee children as 'traumatised and unable to learn' and to have low expectations of them.

- Cultural bias in curriculum content and assessment tasks is compounded by unfamiliarity with text/exam culture.

- Effective home/school links are often lacking. Many parents think their children are doing well simply because they move up a class each year.

Teachers need to be more rigorous in demanding that Somali children work to their full potential. There should also be more effective ethnic monitoring of the academic progress of Somali pupils. Ofsted's *Recent Research in the Achievement of Ethnic Minority Pupils* (Gillborn and Gipps, 1996), the most far-reaching review on its subject for over a decade, made no direct reference to Somali pupils. An important conclusion, nevertheless, arises from the research: that 'Black pupils generally may be falling further behind the average achievement of the majority of their peers.'

The prospect of a disillusioned and underqualified 'under class' has prompted the government to take the issue of underachievement seriously and respond to the needs of ethnic minorities. A 10-point Action Plan has been put in place which includes: the collection of baseline statistics on the ethnic composition of each school; the use of these statistics to monitor ethnic minority pupils' progress through the National Curriculum and the requirement that issues of race are included in initial training of teachers.

The Education Reform Act (1988) failed to take ethnicity and race equality issues into account and most schools have no effective ethnic monitoring system. Categorising different black ethnic groups within the broadly defined 'Black' group can, however, be unhelpful. Somalis and Kenyans, for example, although next-door neighbours, share little by way of linguistic, social and cultural profiles. So the DfEE should review its generic criteria for categorising ethnic groups and adopt a system that takes account of specific ethnic character in terms of national reference.

Somalis have been overlooked in previous research on race and ethnicity on the basis of number and uneven geographical location. At present, in addition to an all-round increase in the numbers of Somalis arriving in the UK, there is an emerging settlement pattern. Cardiff, for example, and the London boroughs of Tower Hamlets, Ealing, Haringey and Newham now have relatively high concentrations of Somalis, which can make such targeted research relevant and meaningful.

Despite the general low achievement, not all is doom and gloom. There are, of course, success stories. There are a good number of Somali children who have done their best against the odds and realised their potential – some have even made it to Oxbridge! In many schools where children do well, Somali children do well too.

Chapter 6

SOMALI GIRLS IN SCHOOLS

Somali girls in schools have particular needs and experiences, which are not recognised. Often they are treated in an identical manner to other bilingual children and their special needs and their status is ignored. Although research work into the educational needs of some immigrant communities, particularly Muslims in Britain (eg Parker-Jenkins, 1995), may have some relevance, such knowledge does not necessarily provide all the insights needed to effectively tackle the educational problems facing Somali girls, which encompass a host of underlying factors embedded in their background and status within Somalia.

In general terms, girls from ethnic minority groups are the least understood of all pupils in school by teachers and pupils alike. They are at the bottom of the hierarchy of power, often marginalised and most vulnerable to stereotyping. They are also the least empowered to understand or intervene in school life or to have any impact on it (Amara, 1984).

Somali girls experience problems that relatively exceed those faced by other ethnic groups or even by their male Somali counterparts. They are likely to have to deal with many, if not all, of the following:

• language and literacy problems

• social and cultural barriers

• problems regarding PE and games

• trauma due to their experience of high intensity civil war

- dual roles at home and school, which create implicit cultural/social dilemmas;

- negative attitudes and low expectations from teachers

- stereotyped views of their cultural values

- female circumcision, and

- sexism and racism.

To repond to the specific background and needs of Somali girls, the following strategies and approaches are recommended.

SINGLE SEX EDUCATION

With the introduction of comprehensive schools in the early sixties, provision for single sex intake within state schools has shrunk. According to the Association of Maintained Girls' Schools (AMGS), the hostility towards single sex education is motivated by political dogma rather than any established educational reasons and arguments. In fact, there is ample evidence that single sex schools lead to higher academic achievement and offer more suitable learning environments as well as appropriate role models for both sexes.

Somali parents generally prefer to send their children, especially their daughters, to single sex schools. Their preference is partly on educational grounds but mostly to ideological opposition to co-educational schooling (see Swann Report, 1985; Parker-Jenkins, 1991). However, single sex state schools are rare and private schooling is beyond the means of almost all Somali parents. Access to private Muslim schools is equally elusive. Somali parents have no option but to look to state schools (comprehensive mixed as a last resort) to accommodate the special needs of their daughters.

Somali society is inherently patriarchal – a male dominated society in which women traditionally play a subordinate role. From an early age, girls are expected to be obedient and passive, deriving their self-worth through family roles, though individual achievement and abilities may be recognized in their own right. Although the Somali community is generally prepared to adapt its views, gender equality is generally given no more than lip-service. Somali parents do, however, place considerable value upon the education of their children – boys and girls alike –

and see themselves as instrumental in ensuring that their children apply themselves fully to school work. All this has implications for classroom practice. Somali girls, particularly in a mixed class, appear uninterested and passive, sitting quietly at the back and hardly contributing to class discussion. Single sex schools stand to provide better opportunities for girls to achieve their full potential as capable and achieving individuals in their own right.

SEX EDUCATION

Unlike Religious Education and Collective Worship, parents do not have the legal right to withdraw their children from sex education. This is at the discretion of the school governors, who also have the right to decide whether or not sex education should be included in the curriculum (ERA, 1988). When parents make a case for withdrawal, school management and governors tend to reject the application outright as uninformed and outdated. Somali parents generally agree that the best environment for providing guidance on sexual matters is the single sex setting: mothers teach their daughters and fathers their sons. Traditionally, Somali parents would teach sex education to their own children as a religious obligation, but not before a certain age when the child is deemed ready to receive it. Somali parents would certainly insist that if sex education must be taught in the school timetable, then it should be by a female teacher for Somali girls above the age of puberty.

For sex education to accommodate the special needs of Somali girls, it is necessary to take into account significant background factors specific to their social and sexual mores. Teachers therefore need to be sensitive when dealing with such controversial topics as safe sex in relation to contraception, so as not to compromise the Muslim stand against sexual experimentation. Such topics need to be put in a moral context and within the framework of traditional family life. Otherwise, requests for withdrawal from sex education lessons should be respected and children given alternative academic work. What is being argued for is not unreasonable or extra, but appropriate and accessible curricular provision.

In many schools, a full copy of the school policy on sex education is available on request and the materials used may be inspected at school. These are with rare exceptions in English so not fully accessible to most Somali parents. Moreover, there is an overlap and some sex education lessons are taught in science and humanities, making it all the more difficult for parents to intervene.

Somali parents must be conscious of their duty and should not shy away from discussing sexual matters with their children. They are also strongly advised to supplement their children's sex education with a specifically Muslim viewpoint (Hassan, 1996).

RACIAL HARASSMENT AND BULLYING

Harassment and bullying are more widespread than is acknowledged. Research (Besag 1989; Elliot, 1986) has identified that at least one in four of any school population has been involved in bullying as a victim or a perpetrator at some point in their school career. Girls appear to use verbal bullying and ostracism as a form of social manipulation: 'bitchiness has become an aggression' (*Times*, 1996). Many Somali girls experience racial taunts and physical bullying; while others talk of being ostracised not only among friendship groups but also along ethnic lines. This exclusion adds to their inherent isolation, made all the more taxing by their being a minority in a class or a school.

Many Somali girls have found themselves on the receiving end of bullying and ostracism. Amina in year 7 in a girls school in West London, for example has experienced both verbal and physical by a group of Asian girls. She told me: 'I was confronted by the same group of Asian girls at the bus stop, who demanded that I should hand over my pocket money. When I failed – as I had none – they began to push and tussle with me and all call me names. On one occasion, they threw my books into a puddle.' (See also Chapter 7, Case B).

Racial and sexual harassment is common in mixed schools. Taunting or physical assaults on account of racial and religious difference is causing concern to many Somali parents, who believe that their daughters are easy targets if they choose to wear the hijab. Dega, now 19 years old and doing an access course at a college in South London, recalls the racial abuse she had to put up with in school: 'As I am Muslim, I had to wear my hijab; but it frequently attracted a range of abuse: racial taunting, disdainful looks, exclusion and at times physical attacks. Being fairly new to the school with little English language, I found the experience pretty traumatising.'

Racial prejudice and racism towards girls is often taken less seriously than among boys because it is relatively less likely to develop into a larger conflict (Amara, 1984). Many Somali girls feel scared and powerless in the face of racial taunts and physical bullying. Their limited command of English often proves a double disadvantage, both attracting abuse and making them unable to seek redress.

It is time schools took a responsible stance over racial harassment and bullying and were prepared to apportion blame and adopt direct strategies for supporting victims.

PHYSICAL EDUCATION

PE and games pose particular problems for Somali girls. It is hardly surprising that such extrovert physical activities are unappealing to Somali girls, who are traditionally self-effacing and embarrassed by attracting any attention to themselves, particularly in mixed company. Their participation is generally reluctant and instances of 'bunking off', feigning illness or injury or 'forgetting' PE kits are not uncommon.

Many Somali object to mixed PE, as it violates their religious practice of forbidding their older girls to mix with unrelated males or to bare their limbs in mixed company. Though it may restrict some timetable options with regard to mixed classes, it is important that alternative arrangements be made, for instance, in swimming lessons.

From a different perspective, a number of Somali girls find themselves in an awkward situation and face real dilemmas when it comes to taking part in games, gymnastics or swimming: it is difficult to keep to the religious teachings about dress and at the same time wear the clothing their classmates wear. The most suitable sportswear for girls is a track suit instead of shorts and vest, as this would respect Islamic modesty. All it calls for is a little understanding and tolerance on the part of the teachers and the other pupils.

Communal showering or being naked in front of others is another contentious issue. Allowing Somali girls to shower earlier than the rest of the class or to wear bathing costumes does not solve the problem. Islam forbids undressing in front of others or being among others who are naked. Unless they provide individual cubicles for changing and showering, schools should permit Somali children to shower at home.

SELF-ESTEEM

Self-esteem is a complex idea intertwined with the concept of identity and can affect educational attainment. Somali girls generally have high self-esteem, emanating from the traditional nomadic culture which underpins a sense of independence and self-assurance. They are also at ease with their physical appearance. This may cushion some of the negative stereotypes attributed by the dominant community to ethnic groups. However, if they feel marginalised at school and their linguistic and cultural background is devalued, their school performance may suffer.

As part of the settlement process, Somali girls have to learn to live with their new minority status. Unlike in their home country, they are presented with few positive images of people from their own background who are in positions of authority. There are very few Somali adults in the teaching or related professions and the few black people they come in frequent contact with in schools are generally doing the cleaning or catering. At micro-level, many girls have high achieving members of their extended, if not immediate, family with whom they can identify and may choose to emulate, but there are seldom key figures in the public spectrum for them to identify with.

DESTINATIONS

No statistics are available in relation to the destinations of Somali girls when they leave school. However, a pilot survey conducted by Somalink (1996) has shown that many Somali girls are relatively poorly qualified but aspire to upward mobility through education and training. A few go directly into higher education and a larger number attend Colleges of Further Education. The majority, however, hope to acquire certain skills, mostly through employment training programmes. In the main, Somali girls are attracted to careers in nursing and in leisure and tourism.

Like many other bilingual children, Somali girls generally lack experience and confidence in telephone/interview skills and in related skills such as writing CVs or arranging references. Children need to be trained in such essential job-search skills if they are to make some headway in going into proper employment.

Somali children need to know about the race equality and sex equality legislation in the UK and its implications for their training and employment.

The educational attainment of Somali girls is relatively better than that of the boys, perhaps because of superior motivation to make the best of the educational opportunities in the host country. Obtaining a National Vocational Qualification (NVQ) and undertaking vocational training are perfectly valid alternatives to the more academic route of taking GCSE and 'A' Levels. However, many Somali girls tend to quit college courses because of the government-set limits on the time claimants can spend on education and training. Those studying more than 21 hours a week forfeit benefit, a life-line for many Somali girls who do not qualify for grants due to residence criteria. The arbitrary interpretation of benefit rules in relation to the 21-hour rule rarely works in their favour and many aspiring young girls on access courses are forced to look for other options. Due to the limited employment opportunities and lack of proper career guidance many end up on the dole.

FEMALE CIRCUMCISION: SACRAMENTAL OR MUTILATING OPERATION?

Circumcision, euphemistically called '*xalaalayn*' in Somali (making clean), is a deeply embedded cultural rite. Male circumcision, dating back to prehistoric times, is a relatively simple and straightforward operation to remove the penile foreskin. It is performed both as a sacrament and as a sanitary measure. Female circumcision – the excision of all or parts of external genitalia – is, however, a mutilating procedure, often involving the removal of the clitoris. According to the Hoskin Report (1993), over 80% of women in Somalia and Djibouti (65% ethnic Somalis) undergo ritualistic genital mutilation. Moreover, the women are infibulated: the two sides of the vulva held together with thorns (in remote rural and nomadic settlements) or sewn together with stitches. A minuscule opening is left for urine and menstruation.

This mutilating ritual usually occurs well before puberty – between the ages of six and ten or even earlier. At present, the operation is carried out by a qualified midwife or nurse but not long ago, especially in rural areas, it was carried out by a traditional circumciser using relatively primitive and unhygenic instruments. The operation was performed without anaesthetic. As the victim writhed in agony, older women held her hands down, legs apart and her mouth shut. The whole operation –

incision and infibulation – could take between 20 to 25 minutes. After the operation, the girl's legs were bound together from knee to ankle to ensure the infibulation stayed in place and this could continue at night for up to two weeks to permit the formation of scar tissue. Urination and menstruation become excruciatingly painful. It can take up to 20 minutes to empty the bladder.

Circumcision deprives women not only of the organs of sexual pleasure but subjects them to hideous pain in urination, menstruation and usually causes multiple medical complications, both immediate and long-term (Dirie and Lindmark, 1992). The first sexual encounter, instead of ushering in a pleasurable conjugal life, is rendered practically unbearable. Consummation may take weeks, with a midwife having to open the infibulation or the husband making repeated efforts to force a penetration.

Many Somali women see pregnancy as an escape from these painful and joyless experiences but childbirth is traumatic. The scar tissue is often ripped open and those women lucky enough to be in urban areas with access to medical attention will be given an episiotomy. In rural areas, maternal mortality runs at roughly 1.1% (UNICEF, 1992). Those who die in their first child-birth do so due to haemorrhage or birth canal obstruction from scar tissue (Mohamoud, 1991). Beyond the danger and the physical pain, there lies the emotional and psychological distress undergone by these young women.

A Pharaonic Practice

The ritual female genital mutilation (FGM) practised in Somalia is traced to the pharaonic period. According to popular Somali mythology, the Pharaohs in ancient Egypt practised infibulation as a sadistic measure to condemn their ex-wives to sexual deprivation. The practice has been going on unabated in Somalia ever since. It has no mandate even in the most strict interpretation of Islamic religion, nor is it based on biological or medical facts; rather, it is based and flourishes on prevalent superstition and religious obscurantism (Abdalla, 1983).

Despite high level observance of the ritual, Somalia has recently seen some determined steps to abolish female infibulation. In the late 1970s, under the leadership of the Somali Women's Democratic Organisation (SWDO) Somali women publicly expressed their abhorrence of this callous ritual. Since then, the official government policy in relation to female circumcision has been to encourage the mildest type: *sunnayn* (Sunnah), which involves the pricking of the clitoris to release a drop of blood. The civil war and subsequent upheaval in the early 1990s, however, drastically hampered this pioneering programme for the eradication of female genital mutilation.

An uncircumcised girl is called *buuryaqab* in Somali. She is traditionally ostracised, labelled 'unclean' and even branded a whore. It is still not uncommon for certain sections of the community to consider marriage to an uncircumcised young woman as a sacrilege and to view her children as bastards. There are many instances in which an unfibulated girl has found it difficult to bear the anxiety and mental torment and opted for the operation (Gallo, 1985). Exclusion from the social ranks of the peer group proved an excruciating form of discrimination. Infibulation used to be an important initiation rite; however, it seems to have lost its symbolism lately and is no longer celebrated with an elaborate or enthusiastic rejoicing ceremony. Girls are nonetheless still prisoners of ritual.

In the Somali culture, virginity is considered an absolute prerequisite for marriage, and chastity is the norm for conjugal harmony. Infibulation is regarded as a means to preserve the girl's virginity and protect her from unbridled passion or promiscuity. Abdi, a Somali social worker in East London disagrees: 'It may well have the opposite effects – lulling the poor girl into a false sense of security or encouraging her to behave naughtily and offer a chance to lead a lose life. It may somehow, however, protect the girl as a rape victim'.

He further commentes: 'Chastity, after all, is spiritual in nature and transcends the physical bounds. From a practical point of view, reinfibulation can easily be done to deceive!'

FGM underlines the contradictions in the attitude and practice of many Somali men. They too often have double standards in relation to virginity and chastity, which are notionally linked to the essence of the practice. It takes more than one to engage in sexual intercourse; it is men who seduce girls and married women. They regard their role as fathers and brothers in an entirely different light from their role as lovers. They want their wives to preserve their chastity but they don't mind having affairs with other women – married or not! They want their daughters to keep their virginity before marriage but don't mind having sex with another girl, Similarly, Somali boys generally feel free to have premarital sex with girls while wanting to marry a virgin. They don't want their sisters to engage in unbridled sexual passion but feel under no obligation to someone else's sister! Such contradictions mask feelings of inadequacy amongst men who secretly fear that uncircumcised women will prove sexually demanding, a particular concern for men in polygamous marriages. Another important cultural consideration is: the traditional Somali view of the woman as a subordinate whose role is within the confines of the home, and on whose moral virtue the family reputation depends.

The situation in the UK

The Somali community has had a visible presence in the UK since the turn of the century or even earlier. In earlier years, the majority of Somali immigrants were men but the late 1980s Somali families arrived and some still continued to excise their daughters, paying a native midwife/nurse or sending the girls to Somalia or the Middle East to have the operation performed.

UK legislation prohibits any procedure of female circumcision. The Prohibition of Female Circumcision Act 1985 also makes it illegal to aid, abet, counsel or procure the carrying out of these procedures. Under the Children Act 1989, female circumcision has been brought within the ambit of child protection but few parents have been committed in the courts. It appears that some parents are exploiting a loophole in the legislation; though in some cases FGM has been prevented by the intervention of the local authority. Recognising that legislation alone would not stop the practice, the focus of anti-FGM groups has been on education, training and counselling for the affected communities so as to encourage prevention and avoid criminalization of the practice.

The social, cultural and religious beliefs that surround the practice of FGM are far too complex and profound to come to a sudden halt with the settlement process in the UK. Khadra, a Somali community worker in Sheffield and a mother of two teenage daughters, expressed her uncertainty and ethical dilemma over the operation: 'I know it is unethical to subject an innocent girl to this barbaric ritual with no apparent medical advantages; but what can you do ... when it is an accepted cultural norm?' True, it takes time for old customs to die out and there needs to be a change in attitude and ideology. On the whole, the tradition is now beginning to disappear, albeit too slowly. S. Dirir, the co-ordinator of London Black Women's Health Action Project, which has been actively campaigning against FGM for well over a decade notes that:

'There have been concerted campaigns both in the UK and in Somalia which appear to have brought the issue of FGM into the public domain. I am encouraged by the growing sentiment in men that the FGM ritual serves no medical, aesthetic or practical purpose and that the human suffering is not acceptable. The practice is now getting less both in scope and intensity. Instead of incision and infibulation, many Somali families now resort to the *Sunnah* version. This is a step in the right direction, but leaves much to be desired.'

Whatever the origins, rationale, or current trends for this ritual, FGM remains a status symbol for women in Somalia and elsewhere in Africa. As Elworthy (1992) notes in her preface to the Minority Rights Group pamphlet – *FGM; Proposals for Change*: 'aspects of sexuality, health, education human rights ... and the rights to development are involved.' Its eradication requires a fundamental transformation of Somali society. Could the current political and social upheaval in Somalia herald the required social transformation?

Implications for schooling

The majority of Somali girls at school have either undergone the *Sunnah* – the mildest type of circumcision – or have been spared but there are some girls from rural backgrounds or from urban families with dogmatic views about circumcision, who have apparently been subjected to FGM.

The general health of these girls is affected. Infibulation causes some medical complications related to menstruation. The minuscule opening that results from infibulation often interferes with the natural flow of bleeding. The blood clots can cause a blockage, which is usually relieved by the use of finger nails accompanied by urine pressure. Some girls suffer from excessive pain which usually starts a day or two before the onset of the bleeding and lasts for several days. It tends to be spasmodic in nature and may be accompanied by nausea or vomiting.

The pinhole opening also interferes with the flow of urine and it takes much longer and causes great discomfort for these girls to empty their bladders. Some teachers may misinterpret time spent in the toilets as loitering or avoiding lessons. Teachers need to be aware of these girls' situation and show care and understanding for their predicament.

It is not uncommon for infibulated girls to be restricted in their agility, whether physically because of heavy keloid scarring or psychologically, for fear of losing their virginity if they perform certain stretches. The excruciating ordeal of menstruation can also affect their general well-being and make physical exercises too demanding for them.

In the Somali tradition, issues of sexuality are usually considered inappropriate for children. Moreover, sexuality issues are rarely discussed in the formal context of the classroom; discussing them in the presence of a member of the opposite sex is generally considered taboo. Lessons that deal with female sexuality may trigger fear and anxiety on the part of infibulated girls, and teachers should handle such topics with sensitivity and understanding.

There is apparently a reversal of status regarding infibulation: whereas in Somalia, the practice is condoned within the cultural milieu, in the UK, it is condemned as an inhumane and mutilating procedure. Girls subjected to FGM may feel outcast in a society where the practice is regarded as barbaric and uncouth. This is likely to create feelings of guilt, betrayal or induce self-doubt in terms of negative physical or personal integrity, thus underminning the girls' self-esteem. Girls face a desperate dilemma if they have gynaecological complications, not knowing whether they dare seek medical help and so risk losing their virginity and with it their future prospects of marriage, or endure the pain in silence.

Some older girls may begin to question the validity of FGM. They may view it as outright breach of their rights to physical and personal integrity and may demand answers. This too may unleash a chain of psychological repercussions: parents may feel guilty or inadequate and the girl may even renounce her culture and family background, with all the alienation this would engender.

Chapter 7

CASE AND PERSONAL HISTORIES

This chapter focuses on selected cases which may provide further insights into the problems and concerns in relation to the education of Somali children. These cases referred to Somali teachers, language assistants, community representatives or parents themselves, across schools in Greater London.

CASE A

A is a boy aged almost ten who joined the school in 1994. He is the youngest of a family of four in this country. He is looked after by an older sister. Other family members including both parents are in a refugee camp in Ethiopia. The school is concerned about A because his development is in many ways poor.

He often seems distressed and distracted. He can be very aggressive and is unable to share, co-operate or play with his peer group. He is always arguing and fighting in class and the playground. A's behaviour is generally very immature and egocentric. Though he constantly seeks attention, he is often reluctant to co-operate with adults. His concentration and listening skills are poor and this has impeded his acquisition of English. Furthermore, he distracts other children. He shows no interest in books; his hand control is poor and he needs constant one-to-one attention to produce any kind of work.

A manifests behaviour patterns consistent with emotionally traumatised children. He is aggressive and easily irritable and finds it difficult to settle in and concentrate. His situation was further exacerbated by the sudden exposure to a daunting school environment for which he was not prepared. He was born and brought up in a nomadic settlement, has had no experience of formal school, no experience of urban life and his social interaction is confined to family members.

A appears to be missing his other family members. Lack of parental affection and care has definitely had negative effects on his social and emotional development and, by extension, upon his learning and progress. A would benefit from a flexible age grouping where he could stay with the same teacher for two years to slowly gain confidence and acquire basic language and literacy skills.

A would also benefit from pastoral care and guidance, preferably from a bilingual teacher/language assistant, to enable him to adapt to the formal learning environment. Above all, he needs attention, understanding and affection for his emotional and social development.

CASE B

B has been in this country for two years and is in year 9. On several occasions, B has arrived late to lessons/registration. He is finding it difficult to settle into school or to behave in an appropriate manner, both in and out of lessons. He has used excuses such as not having his timetable or getting lost. In his second year at school, one would expect B to know these things and to use his diary to remind him of his timetable. In lessons, B is making little progress. He spends a great deal of time day-dreaming. Without frequent prompting, he produces very little work. He has language difficulties but sometimes uses this as an excuse for not doing work.

B was subjected to continual racial abuse and bullying by a group of boys in his class. On one occasion they took his pocket money away and broke a new pen his mother had bought him. He informed his class teacher but no action was taken, even though he had been instructed that he should report such incidents. He once fought back and scratched a boy and was then suspended for two days. B felt fearful and intimidated and began to dread coming to school. Finally, he informed his mother and the matter was referred to the headteacher. To the family's disgust, the headteacher trivialised their complaint as a classroom matter and no action was taken. Both pupil and parent have lost trust in the school and the mother has decided to transfer her son to another school.

Somali children speak of a general experience of racial harassment ranging from verbal abuse and bullying to physical attacks both inside and outside school. Indirect bullying – more sinister and damaging in social and emotional terms than physical and verbal bullying – often takes the form of excluding them from formal classroom groupings as well as informal social groups. Somali parents are concerned about schools' indifference to the plight of their children who suffer bullying and racial harassment.

CASE C

C is in year 10 in a secondary school. He arrived in this country in 1994 straight from Somalia. C is the eldest of a family of seven. His father is still stranded in Somalia. The school is concerned about C's casual attitude to school attendance. On average, C misses at least one day a week of school; sometimes three or four, and is more often late than on time. He has begun to play truant. C is given a great deal of support during the week and the school is peturbed about his casual attitude to school.

C finds his school work far too difficult. He knows that with his limited language and literacy level, he is likely to end up in year 11 with no exam passes and no hope of getting any qualifications. His sense of failure may breed disillusionment and resentment against a system he feels is not taking him anywhere. He may try to reduce the effects of the negative experience at school by adopting an apathetic attitude and playing truant.

C is acting as a surrogate father, taking his brother and sisters to school or to their GP or hospital appointments. His apparent new role seems at variance with his educational pursuit but it gives him a sense of achievement and satisfaction.

CASE D

> **D** was admitted to school at the age of nine. She arrived in England in
> early 1994 from a refugee camp in Kenya. She is the eldest of a family
> of five. All members of her immediate family are here in London but
> extended family members who were living with her in the same house
> in Mogadishu are still in the refugee camp. **D** is quite timid and shy.
> When she was brought to school, she looked ill: emaciated, rather
> small for her age and physically slow. After a term, **D** was appeared
> extremely insecure. She talked very little but was obedient and well
> behaved. She did not interact with the children in her class and was not
> interested in any work or games.

The school realised that **D** needed specialist help which it was not
equipped to give. Immediate referral was made to the educational
psychologist. Consultation sessions revealed that the child was
extremely close to her grandmother and separation is causing **D**
traumatic stress. In Somalia, the extended family is the norm and
children are used to different carers within it. The child's age was
wrongly recorded by her uncle, who submitted an application for
family reunion on their behalf from London, and she is actually a year
and half younger than the age given on the Home Office documents.

To the dismay of the school, there was little they could about **D**'s
unhappy situation. The LEA was quite adamant about the age issue. The
official LEA stance was that the child should be educated in her 'year'
group and they insisted that unless her documents were amended by the
Home Office, there was nothing they could do. The family was obliged
to make the next move: to go to the Home Office and ask to amend the
date of birth. This looked straightforward but proved to be difficult and
complicated in the light of their circumstances. Would this interfere
with their application for a family reunion to get the grandmother to
come over to England, they wondered? They thought it might be a good
idea to wait for the application to be processed and postpone the age
issue. But an application for family reunion usually takes between one
and two years to be processed and judging from the latest statistics, the
chances of an acceptance are pretty slim. The suffering of child **D**
continues, along with the evident frustration of the school.

An important practical issue which deserves mention is the way of recording ages. Under normal circumstances, it is not difficult to record ages accurately and give the correct date of birth. But the displacement and subsequent transit or resettlement process can lead to discrepancies or confusion. As a desperate measure to circumvent immigration control, one may be tempted to alter the date of birth or an applicant who has submitted an application for family reunion could make a genuine mistake. Moreover, a false date may be thought to be in the best interest of a child, either to ensure that s/he has an extra year or two of schooling or not to risk refusal to school on grounds of age.

The emotional energy of **D**'s parents to support her is depleted by their own suffering from loss, guilt and shame. In Mogadishu one night, a gang of looters stormed into their house and butted her father unconscious, raped her mother and in the mayhem shot dead a year-old baby – all in front of **D,** who was almost eight. The death of the baby has left both parents mentally scared, filled with a sense of guilt and feelings of betrayal. They are left on their own to cope with that sense of loss and shame, with no access to professional counselling. In a futile effort to forget the past and plan for the future, the father passes his time chewing qat – but the leaves merely induce obsessive reflection of the past and irrational charting of the future. Moreover, qat can cause insomnia, loss of appetite, lethargy, dramatic mood swings and may even trigger psychotic disorders. Poor **D** is lost in an environment suffused with feelings of guilt and foreboding and with no a sense of purpose or direction.

CASE E

E arrived in the UK in early 1993 from Somalia, aged fifteen. She had five years of formal but erratic schooling in Somalia. On arrival, she was put on an intensive language course. Teachers were impressed with her academic progress but concerned about her social development. E could not fit in with the children in the withdrawal group or in her tutor group. She always kept her distance and was at times moody and unwilling to take part in any group work. Her behaviour and social outlook suggested a remarkable maturity and she found it easy to relate to adults. Physically, E looked much older than she claimed; but in any case, it was difficult to ascertain her age.

E's school work was generally good and she was recommended to return to her mainstream class at the end of the term. Things then went downhill. E's attendance, which was already far from satisfactory, got worse. She began to excuse herself from school almost every other day. Sometimes, she would not turn up for a week. Letters were sent home and her parents were sent for; but to no avail. Finally, a bilingual teacher's home visit established that E had left for Manchester and had no plan to come back to the school.

E was in fact older than her Home Office documents showed – nearly twenty years old. She was the only surviving member of a family of five who had perished in the indiscriminate artillery shelling of Hargeisa in early 1988. Her uncle decided to take her to England with his family as a last minute replacement for his teenage daughter who had died of malaria a month earlier.

E could not fit into her withdrawal and tutor groups. She could not socialise and relate to children who were so much younger – in some cases by seven or eight years. Moreover, she has an introvert personality that could add to her classroom inhibition and anxiety.

E tried to leave school early and applied to a number of colleges, who gave her a conditional offer – but her age was always an obstacle. She tried to explain her predicament to her uncle but he was not prepared to do anything that might jeopardise his family's stay in the country.

E was sad, frustrated and totally confused. She could go to the Home Office and explain the situation but they would not listen to her. In any case, she would need an affidavit to ascertain her age and identity. A community leader or an adult relative is required to undertake such a task. No one, however, was willing to get involved in these sensitive family affairs. As a last resort, E decided to get married to get away from this ambivalent situation. She now lives in Manchester with her husband and baby daughter.

AUTOBIOGRAPHICAL STORIES

There follows a selection of autobiographical stories and personal accounts by Somali children. As well as being a source of first-hand evidence of the experience of Somali children, these accounts can provide a practical focus for discussion of issues of personal and social relevance in PSE lessons and other cross-curricular and school-based activities.

The stories have been transcribed as they were written by the pupils.

NIMOA (age 14 years old)
A BORDER TOO FAR

I left Somalia in August 1988. First of all, there was fighting, shooting and shelling. I was in my home sleeping and then I got up and asked my aunt what had happened and she said: 'Don't worry about what happened – just let's get out of the house'. 'Where is mum and dad?' I asked. She said they were outside. Before that day, the neighbours came to us and asked if they could stay in our house today and tomorrow. My mum and dad said that was fine with us because they were so scared and thought they might die.

The next day, the neighbours said to my mum: 'We've to go back to our house and have some food.' As they went back, a soldier was fired at and he thought that the shooting was coming from the neighbours. He then opened fire at their house. The whole family was killed including five children and their pregnant mother. One eleven year old boy survived, and my aunt lied to him and said nothing had happened and told him to come with us. The same people tried to kill us and we all cried and so the commanding officer came and said: 'Leave him alone – he has a lot of children.' The same man said: 'Don't go back – just run!'

So we ran with no shoes. It was raining. It was about four o'clock in the morning. My mum was with our next door neighbours. We had to go somewhere between Somalia and Ethiopia. My aunt said: 'There is a lot of fighting – just come with me.' We thought my mum had died and we were all upset. My mum came at about six o'clock with my aunt. Three days later, we settled in a place far from Hargeisa. We made a little hut from tree branches. It was hot during the day and very cold at night. We had no blankets and no clothes to change into.

One morning, four men came to uncle and asked if he would like to join and fight against the enemy soldiers. They were lying – they were the enemy. They killed my uncle with a knife. He had a wife and a son who was three years old.

Every morning we had to go outside to hide under the tree because of the aeroplanes. Nobody had to wear white or red clothes and no cooking except in the middle of the night. There was not enough water at that time and we had to walk a long distance to fetch water. A lot of people died on their way to or from the stream.

After a few months, we decided to cross the border to Ethiopia. It was no longer safe to be in Somalia. Everybody – about two hundred people with lots of donkeys and camels to carry their stuff – had to be quiet to cross the border. But some people were talking. My mum asked my dad: 'Is this a house?' No. it wasn't a house; it was a tank! They gunned down about half of the people and we had to go back to a place called Anayo, where my youngest sister was born. We had to stay there for a few more months.

One day, me and my aunt had to hide under a tree and we a saw a man with two donkeys. We thought it was the enemy to kill us; but it was my uncle and we were surprised and really happy. He said we had to cross the border tonight. At about three o'clock in the morning, we began our long journey. It rained heavily that day. Next morning, we came to Ethiopia with my whole family. We felt happy and safe at last.

When we arrived my dad had to go to another country called Djibouti. He went to another man to phone my uncle in England. My dad asked my uncle to send us money and visas to come to England. On the way back, the enemy saw my dad and took him to jail. We waited for him to come back but he didn't come. We couldn't find him for two years. Some people said he had died.

Now, my mum had to go to Djibouti to talk to our uncle. My uncle was shocked to hear what had happened and he promised to send us money and visas so that we could join him in England. He told mum to leave the refugee camp at Harta Sheikh and come to Dire Dawa.

One month later, my uncle came to fetch us. We left Dire Dawa to Addis Ababa and we stayed there a few weeks. We then caught a plane to England. It was strange to be on the plane. I felt dizzy and sick.

One day, my dad phoned us in Hounslow West. How happy we all were to hear his voice – we couldn't believe it. We thought he was dead like my other uncle. My dad was in Sweden but he did not know where the plane was going and he asked the Somali people on board: 'Where are we now?' They all laughed! 'You don't know where you are!' But he didn't care: he was happy and thought it was the end of his trouble and, indeed, it was.

Every morning, my dad had to go to the British Embassy in Sweden and tell them he had nine children and a wife in England, but they didn't believe him. Then they phoned my uncle and he said: 'Yes, it's true.' They gave my dad a free ticket and a travel document. We had no idea he was coming. He didn't tell us anything. Perhaps he wanted to make it a surprise – and it really was a surprise. I opened the door and it was dad! We all cried, but inside we were happy.

YUSSUF (now aged 17)
MY FIRST WEEKS AT SCHOOL

My name is Yussuf and I come from Somalia. I was born in Mogadishu, the capital. I started school when I was six. It was a big school but you happened to know each other. I studied in Somali, my mother-tongue. I came to England in 1991 with my older brother. My parents, both very old, decided to stay behind in the war-torn city of Mogadishu. They said they were too old to go to a foreign country. I also have another younger brother and an older sister – married with three children – who are now in Canada. When the war broke out in Mogadishu, we fled across the border to Kenya. We stayed in a refugee camp for six months. Life was very hard there – sometimes there was no food – but we had some peace.

When I first arrived in England, I didn't speak a word of English. Within two weeks, I was put in a secondary school in Newham. It was a very big school with many pupils. They were all boys. I was put in year 8. I remember the first weeks in school were just like hell. I couldn't understand or talk to anybody. There were a number of Somali children but they were in different classes. We met only at lunch time or after school. In the classroom, I could only sit and look at the teachers talking. Some teachers talked slowly; but others were talking fast and teaching us a lot. I couldn't understand the subject so I just sat there in most lessons with no idea what was going around me. I liked PE most because I could take part in some of the activities. I liked football and basket-ball. Sometimes, I had to copy out something from the board or from a book or draw and colour a picture. I didn't like doing these sort of things. They were really boring and a bit childish.

Sometimes children, especially bad kids, picked on me. They knew I was new to school and didn't speak English. They used to take the mickey out of me and sometimes went further by calling me names and making racial taunts. I knew they were up to mischief, but what could you do? They could carry on winding you up till you lost your temper and at times you got physical. I remember one day I pushed one stupid boy who made it habit to make fun of me. The day before, the same bad boy tripped me over and I fell down and hurt my shoulder. The teacher saw me push him and I was given detention. It was very frustrating when you aren't able to tell your side of the story. These naughty boys were quite clever to pretend their innocence and you got punished for something you hadn't done.

At times, you couldn't help but hate and curse yourself for not being able to express yourself and explain to the teacher what had happened. One day, a boy tripped me over and I fell down and hit my knees on a concrete tennis court. I thought about hitting him but I decided against it. I went straight to the form tutor to report the incident. I could not tell him anything more than the name of the boy and showing him the graze on my knees. The teacher was kind and began to encourage me to say more; but I couldn't. I felt sad for not being able to express myself and angry that these idiots are taking advantage of my situation.

SAHRA (age 14)
I WANT MY MOTHER

My name is Sahra. I am fourteen years old. I was born in April 1981 in Somalia. I have a mother but I haven't got a father – he was shot dead by a soldier near our house in Hargeisa. I have three brothers and four sisters. We are not all here in England; only one brother and one sister and me are in England. We are looked after by my aunt. My mum and other brothers and sisters are in a camp between Somalia and Ethiopia.

Not long ago, we were a happy family and relatively well off; but now we are not. We lost our dad and our mum is not here with us. We want our mum to come here; but it is not possible – she hasn't got a visa. When the war started in Hargeisa, we were in our house. You couldn't go out because there were soldiers everywhere who would shoot you. All the shops and schools were closed.

One day, my father went to visit my grandma who was living with my aunt in another part of the city. On his way back, the soldiers shot him near our house. We all cried and couldn't stop. Everyday, people got killed, houses searched for SNM fighters and destroyed. There were big explosions all around us and planes were flying high up in the sky and throwing bombs. We could no longer live in our house and decided to flee across the border to Ethiopia. We ran away in the night. All my family left, apart from my father and sister who had been killed.

With some of our neighbours, we walked for three weeks. We hid ourselves in the bush during the night and walked through the night. Some people didn't have any shoes or warm clothes. Some of us had no shoes. We walked through the east of Ethiopia to Mogadishu. We stayed there for two and half years, but then the fighting broke out in Mogadishu. We had to run away to the Kenyan border. There, we split up. My mum, two brothers and three sisters went Ethiopia. My aunt, one brother and a sister and myself went to Kenya. We lived there for about six months until a distant uncle helped us to come to England.

When I came to England, it was very difficult for me because I couldn't speak English. I started school in Hammersmith. I wanted to learn English and work hard. When I finish school, I would like to become an air hostess. I want to earn money to get my mother over here with us.

SHAMIS (18 years old)
IN THE WAR ZONE

It is now well over 8 years since we left Somalia. It seems a long time, but what happened is still vivid in my mind. I was ten years old when the fighting broke out in my country. No one could stay in the war zone, so I fled with my family. Our country was ruled by a military dictator. He destroyed everything and killed anyone who opposed his rule. There was no freedom of speech, no security and everyone was a suspect. After Siad Barre had ruled Somalia fore almost twenty years, the people rose in revolt and formed an armed movement. After a few years, the group was strong enough to fight against Siad Barre's powerful army.

The fighting started quickly and soon spread all parts of Hargeisa. It was frightening and we were all very worried. We were a large family with many of our aunts staying with us. It started in the middle of the night in May 1988. The army were panicking and were shelling and shooting everywhere. I saw many innocent people killed in front of me, some as young as babies. There was chaos everywhere. People were running in every direction for safety, but there was nowhere safe. There were lots of children who were left alone, crying for help. The war went on for two weeks, non-stop. There was no food or water.

The government was at war with its people and used all its fire-power to destroy the city. The roads were filled with landmines, the bridges were destroyed and the big buildings were blown up. The soldiers were going into every house, searching and stealing any valuables. There were lots of young children who became deaf, and they were so badly shocked that they couldn't speak. I felt frightened and I was shaking, wondering if would die. Dead bodies were all around me and the shrieks and wailing of women and children were echoing around us. Death and destruction were everywhere.

The last day we were going out of the country, we saw corpses lying on the roads. When we were nearly out of the country and into safety, the car in front of us was blown up by a landmine, killing all the passengers.

On the way out, some soldiers stopped our car and said if we didn't pay them money, then they would blow up our car. My dad had to pay almost half of the money we had so they would let us go out of the country to safety.

After a long and tiring journey on a rough and dusty road, we finally reached Djibouti. The control people didn't let us out so we had to wait for about a year. It was very hot and humid and you could hardly sleep even when the fan was on.

When I came to England, I went to a school in Tower Hamlets. It is difficult when you are in a secondary school in a new country. The school was horrible because the children there swore at me and started to fight with me for no reason. It could be that they hated me because I was come from another country and could not speak English very well. Some girls even tried to force me to smoke or play truant. On the whole, it was a pretty distressing experience and finally I decided not to come back to school. Fortunately, my dad was quite understanding and he arranged a transfer to another school in the borough.

CONCLUSION

Despite experiencing a host of difficulties, Somali children are fully committed to their studies, have high ambitions and aspire to get professional qualifications at higher level. Their parents, too, have positive attitudes and expectations of their children and would like them to go into higher education. They arrived with high expectations and high hopes. Much of this hope is focused on their children. Both pupils and parents have high regard and respect for schools and teachers. More importantly, they are very appreciative of the understanding and accommodating spirit accorded to them. It is heartening to see that most of the Somali children have already settled down, adjusted to the school routine and no longer regard school as threatening and daunting; rather, it is now a challenging, stimulating and rewarding experience.

To conclude on a positive note, it may be helpful to refer to a case-study of a remarkable Somali boy who, despite difficult circumstances, persevered to work to his potential and achieved real success in his academic pursuit.

Ahmed is 12 years old. He arrived in the UK in early 1987 straight from Somalia. He was born and brought up in a small rural village in north-west Somaliland. Ahmed has never been to a formal school and had very limited urban experience before coming to England. He is not literate in Somali but knows some Arabic acquired through informal instruction.

Ahmed is part of a dispersed family. Both parents and two sisters are in Somaliland, and an older sister is married in Saudi Arabia. Ahmed shares a bed-sit with an older brother in a hostel run by the Refugee Council. He is on Income support and finds it difficult to make ends meet on the meagre budget.

At home, he has no support to guide and help him in his studies; no parent to instil a vision of achievement. Ahmed is amazingly cheerful, considering all that he has had to go through.

It would seem at the outset that Ahmed did not stand a realistic chance of achieving good grades in his GCSE, let alone attempt A-level courses. With his limited language and literacy levels of English, the odds are stacked against him. However, through sheer hard work and determination, Ahmed has proved all his doubters wrong and achieved good exam results: 8 GCSEs with grades A-C. Now he is in his second year in college doing A-levels.

This has not happened in isolation; but in the context of a school – a school with an integrated approach to education, a caring pastoral system, committed to academic achievement and constructive in its community links. With appropriate support, Somali children can be equipped to make a positive contribution to the country that has given them refuge.

GLOSSARY

Beginner: A bilingual pupil with little or no knowledge of English. A new arrival with little or no formal schooling is categorised as 'Total Beginner'.

Bilingual: Someone developing competence in more than one language (for example in Somali and English). The term does not indicate the competence with which any of the languages is spoken.

CA: Contrastive Analysis – a mode of enquiry in second language acquisition that focuses on the similarities and differences between two languages.

EAL: English as an Additional Language – teaching approaches designed to help bilingual children who do not have good command of English.

First Stage Learner: a bilingual pupil who can take part in classroom activities using their first language.

Gu': The spring season, heaviest rainfall in Somalia

GNP. Gross National Product

GDP: Gross Domestic Product

GCSE: General Certificate of Secondary Education

GEST: Grants for Education Support and Training

Halal: lawful, permissable; (of food and its preparations, sale etc.) conforms to Islamic law.

Haram: unlawful, prohibited.

In-class support: support provided for targeted pupils by an EAL teacher/assistant working within the mainstream class.

INSET: In-service Education and Training.

Juma'a Prayer: The Friday Congregational Prayer which takes the place of Zuhur (mid-day) prayer. Friday is not a holy day as such or compulsory day of rest and worshippers may disperse and go about their business and other activities.

LEA: Local Education Authority

L1: First language or mother tongue.

L2: second language, acquired after L1

Mainstream lesson: the normal classroom base, in which most of the class work takes place.

Meher: witnessed Somali marriage; dowry-payment (in cash or kind) to the bridegroom's family.

PE: Physical Education

PSE: Personal and Social Education

Qur'an: The Muslim holy book, written in Arabic containing the word of Allah (SWT) as revealed to Prophet Mohammed(s).

RE: Religious Education.

Reer: group of people; a nomadic encampment.

Salat: Prayer; the second Pillar of Islam Prayer. Muslims are required to pray five times a day.

SACRE: Standing Advisory Council on Religious Education – established by the Education Reform Act (1988), SACREs advise their local education authority on Religious Education and collective worship.

SATs: Standard Assessment Tasks – formal assessment under the National Curriculum at the Key Satges 7, 11 and 14 in the three core subjects – English, Maths and Science.

SEN: Special Educational Needs, learning difficulties as defined in the Education Acts of 1981 and 1993.

Shari'ah: The moral and legal code of Islam. The two main sources are the Qur'an and the Sunnah (see below) of Prophet Mohammed.

Sunnah: Literally, path or example. Here, it refers in particular to the example of Prophet Mohammed(s) and includes what he said, what he did or agreed to.

SLA: Second Language Acquisition.

SNM: Somali National Movement – formed in 1981 in London as an opposition group to the military regime in Somalia; supported mainly by the Isaq clan.

SSDF: Somali Salvation Democratic Front – formed in 1982 as armed opposition group; operates in Central Somalia and supported mainly by the Majerteen Clan.

Second Stage Learner: A bilingual pupil with fairly developed oral English but with limited literacy level. Can take part in most classroom activities.

Third Stage learner: A bilingual pupil whose oral and written English is developing relatively well. Can participate in most lessons but may need support in more academic work.

USC: United Somali Congress, formed in 1989 in Central Somalia to overthrow Siad Barre regime and now supported mainly by Habar-Gidir of the Hawiye clan.

UNOSOM: United Nations Operation in Somalia – initially, established in early 1992, UNOSOM II took over from UNITAF (see above).

UNITAF: United Nations Task Force – a contingent of multi-national force under the US command.

Withdrawal work: support provided for targeted pupils by EAL teacher or assistant in a separate location from mainstream classroom.

Wadaad: sheikh; religious leader or teacher.

Waranle: laity; literally, one who carries a spear, referring to a warrior.

Xeer: treaty; law; social or legal contract.

BIBLIOGRAPHY

Abdalla, R (1983) *Sisters in Affliction: Circumcision and Infibulation in Africa*, Uppsala: Scandinivian Institute of African Studies.

Adam, H M (1968) A Nation in Search of a Script, (MA thesis), University of Makerere

Adam, H M (1980) 'The Revolutionary Development of the Somali Language', *African Studies Centre Occasional Paper Series* 20, Los Angeles, University of California.

Aden, S (1995) 'Educating Somali Children'. Talk given at a Somali Awareness Training Day at Hounslow Civic Centre.

Africa Watch (1990) *Somalia: A Government at War with its People*, London: Human Rights Watch.

Ahmed, S (1996) *Khat and illicit drug use amongst the Somali community in Tower Hamlets*, London: Liban Project

Alladina, S and Edwards V (1991) *Multilingualism in the British Isles, Africa, the Middle East and Asia*, London: Longmans

Amara, N (1984) 'An Alien Environment' *Issues for Girls*, London: Issues in Race and Education

Andrzejeweski, B W (1963) 'Poetry in Somali Society', *New Society*, 25, 22-24

Andrzejeweski, B W and Lewis, I M (1964) *Somali poetry*, Oxford:Oxford University Press

Ayotte, W (1995) *No Refuge for Children*, London: Save the Children.

Baker, A M (1990) 'The Psychological Impact of the Intifada on Palestinian Children in the Occupied West Bank and Gaza: An Exploratory Study,' *American Journal of Orthopsychiatry* 60, 496-505

Baker, C (1995) *A Parent's and Teacher's Guide to Bilingualism*, London: Multinlingual Matters

Bahafunzi, B (1996) 'The Education of the Bravanese Community: Key issues of culture and identity', *Educational Studies*, Vol.22, No.3

Bastiani, J (1989) *Working with Parents: a whole-school approach*, London: Routledge

Besag, V (1989) *Bullies and Victims in Schools*, Oxford: Oxford University Press

Bonnet, C (1993) 'The silence of Croatia's children', *International Children Rights Monitor* 10, 3, 12-15

Burton, R (1856) *First Footsteps in East Africa*, (ed) Waterfield, G (1966) London: Routledge

Cassanelli, L V (1982) *The Shaping of Somali Society: Reconstructing the History of Pastoral People 1500-1900*, Pennsylvania: Pennsylvania University Press

Cassnanelli, L V (1994) 'History and Identity Among Somali Refugees: A Recent Example from Coastal Kenya'. Paper presented to the Folklore Seminar, University of Pennsylvania, January, 1994

Cassanalli, L (1995a) 'Explaining the Somali Crisis,' in Besteman, C and Cassanelli L (eds) *The War for Land in Southern Somalia*, Boulder, Col: Westview Press.

Cassanelli, L (1995b) *Victims and Vulnerable Groups in Southern Somalia*, Ottawa: Research Directorate

Coehlo, E (1994) 'Social Integration of Immigrant and Refugee Children', in Genesee, F (ed) *Educationg Second Language Children*, New York: Cambridge University Press.

Collier, V (1989) Age and Rate of Acquisition of Second Language for Academic Purposes, *TESOL Quarterly*, 21, 617-641.

Cummins, J (1981) 'Age on Arrival and Immigrant Second Language in Canada: a reassessment', *Applied Linguistics*, 2, 132-149

Cummins, J (1984) *Bilingualism and Special Education: Issues in Assessment and Pedagogy*, Clevedon: Multilingual Matters

Cummins, J and Swain, M. (1986) *Bilingualism in Education*, New York: Longman

Charter, D (1996) 'Girl Bullies of the Nineties', *The Times*, May 24, 1996

Collins, S (1957) *Coloured Minorites in Britain*, London: Lutterworth Press

Dihod, O – Somali Counselling Project (1996) 'Mental Illness in the Somalis'. Personal Interview

Department for Education and Science (1989) *The Education Reform Act 1988: Religious Education and Collective Worship*, Circular No 389

Department for Education and Science (1989) *English for Ages 5 to 16* (The Cox Report), London, HMSO

Dirie, M and Lindmark, G (1992) 'The Risk of Medical Complications after Female Circumcision', *East Africa Medical Journal*, 69(9), 479-482

Drysdale, J (1991) *Somaliland: Anatomy of Secession*, London: Globe-States Ltd

Drysdale, J (1991) *Somaliland 1991: Report and Reference*, London: Globe-States Ltd

Elworthy, C (1992) in Dorkenno, F and Elworthy, C, *Female Genital Mutilation: Proposals for Change*, London: Minority Rights Group.

Fitzpatrick, F (1987) *The Open Door*, Clevedon: Multilingual Matters.

El-Sohl, C F (1991) 'Somalis in London's East End', *New Community*, 17(4), 539-552

Gallo, P (1985) 'Female Circumcision in Somlia: Some Psychological Aspects', *Genus* 41(11-2), 133-147.

Gillborn, D (1990) *Race, Ethnicity and Education: Teaching and Learning in Multi-ethnic Schools*, London: Unwin Hyman

Gillborn, D and Gipps, C (1996) *Recent Research on the Achievement of Ethnic Minority Pupils*, London: Office for Standards in Education.

Gilkes, P (1994) *Conflict in Somalia and Ethiopia*, London: Wayland

Gimson, A C (1984) *An Introduction to Pronunciation of English*, London: Arnold

Hall, D (1995) *Assessing the Needs of Bilingual Pupils*, London: Fulton

Hamers, J and Blanc, M (1989) *Bilinguality and Bilingualism*, Cambridge: Cambridge Unversity Press.

Home Office Statistical Bulletin 15/95, *Asylum Statistics United Kindom 1994*, London: Government Statistical Service.

Hosken, F (1993) The Hosken Report: Genital and Sexual Mutilation of Females, New York: Women's International Network News

Hunter, F M (1880) *A Grammar of the Somali Language*, Bombay: Education Society's Press

Hassan, A H (1995) Personal communication, December 1995, a Somali teacher in West London

Hassan, A H (1997) *Parental Role in the Education of Somali Children*, forthcoming

Johnson, J W (1974) *Heelooy Heeleelooy: the development of the Genre Heelo in modern Somali Poetry*, Indiana: Red Sea Press

Kinzie, J et al (1989) 'A Three year follow up of Cambodian young people traumatised as children, *The Children: Journal of the American Academy of Child Psychiatry*, 25, 370-376

Klein, R (1994) 'Survivors with hidden scars of war' *Times Educational Supplement*, February, 25, 1994

Lamberti, M (1981) *Map of the Somali Dialects in the Somali Democratic Republic*, Hamburg: Buska

Laitin, D (1992) 'Somalia' *Colliers Encyclopaedia* (1994), vol. 21, 201-203.

Lawrence, M (1954) *A Tree for Poverty: Somali Poetry and Prose*, Nairobi: Eagle Press

Lewis, I M (1961) *A Pastoral Democracy*, Oxford: Oxford University Press (reprint, 1982 , New York: Africana Publishing Company).

Lewis, I M (1988) *A Modern History of Somalia: nation and state in the Horn of Africa*, Boulder: Westview Press

Lewis, I M (1993a) *Understanding Somalia*, London: Haan

Lewis, I M (1993b) *Blood and Bone: the call of kinship in Somali society*, Lawrenceville, NJ: Red Sea Press.

Lewis, I M (1987) 'Somalia', *The World Book Encyclopaedia*, vol. 18, 478-480.

Little, K L (1948) *Negroes in Britain*, London: Trubner and Co

Luling, V (1995) 'Somalia: an update' *Encyclopaedia Britannica Book of the Year*, Chicage: Encyclopedia Britannica

Mohamed, M and Kahin, M (1996) *The Employment and Training Needs of the Somali Community in Brent and Harrow*, London: Somalink

Mohamed, O (1991) 'Female Circuscision and Child Mortality', *Genus* 47(3-4), 203-233.

Punamaki, R L (1988) 'Psychological Reactions of Palestinian and Israeli Children to War and Violence' in Kahnert, S, Pitt, D, Taipalr, I (eds) *Children and War*, Helsinki

Orwin, M (1995) *Colloquial Somali: A complete language course*, London: Routledge

Parker-Jenkins, M (1991) 'Muslim Matters: the Educational Needs of the Muslim child', *New Community*, 17(4), 569-582.

Parker-Jenkins, M (1995) *Children of Islam*, Stoke-on-Trent: Trentham Books

Power *et al* (1995) *No Place to Learn: Homelessness and Education*, London: Shelter.

Richards, J (1971) *Error Analysis and Second Language Strategies*, London: Language Science

Rutter, J (1994) *Refugee Children in the Classroom*, Stoke-on-Trent: Trentham Books

Saeed, J (1987) *Somali Reference Grammar*, London: Wheaton

Sahnoun, M (1994) *Somalia: the missed opportunity*, New York: Westview

Samater, S (1982) *Oral Poetry and Somali Nationalism*, Cambridge: Cambridge University Press.

Samater, S (1991) *A Nation in Turmoil*, London: Minority Rights Group

Schels, C (1992) 'Birdwatching in Somalia', *Journal of the Anglo-Somali Society*, Spring, 1992

Skutnub-Kangas, T (1984) *Bilingualism or not: The Education of Minorities*, Clevedon: Multilingual Matters

Somalink (1996) Destinations of Somali children, Unpublished research work. London, Somalink.

Swann, M (1985) *Education for All: A summary of the Swann Report on the Education of Ethnic Minority Children*, Windsor: NFER-Nelson

UNICEF (1992) *The State of the World's Children*, Oxford University Press

UNDP (1994) *Human Development Report*, Oxford University Press

Verma, G K (1986) *Ethnicity and Educational Achievement*, Basingstoke: Macmillan

Warner, R (1992) 'Loss and grief in the lives of newly arrived bilingual children', *Multicultural Teaching* 10.2, 10-14

DIRECTORY OF SOMALI COMMUNITY ORGANISATIONS IN LONDON

BARNET

Barnet Somali Community Group
156 Golders Green Road
London NW11 8HF
Tel: 0181 731 7588

Somali Self-help and Welfare Association
19 Hemswell Drive
Colindale
London NW9 5WN
Tel: 0181 205 3007

Horn of Africa Women's and Children's Association
21 Hemswell Drive
Colindale
London NW9 5WN
Tel: 0181 205 3007

BRENT

Brent Somali Community Organisation
372 Greenrig Walk
Chalkhill Estate
Wembley
HA9 9UL
Tel: 0181 904 3985

Somali Community of North-west London,
373 Greenrig Walk,
Chalkhill Estate,
Wembley,
HA9 9UL
Tel: 0181 908 6274

Stonebridge Somali Centre
148 Haskel House
Shakespeare Crescent
Stonebridge
London NW10 8DJ
Tel: 0181 904 3958

CAMDEN

Somali Community and Relief Association
Camden Vac
Instrument House
207/215 Kings Cross Road
London WC1X 90B
Tel: 0171 837 5544

Somali Cultural Centre
Kingsgate Community Centre
107 Kingsgate Road
London NW6
Tel: 0171 328 9480

EALING

Ealing Somali Welfare and Cultural Association
Northfields Community Centre
Northcroft Road
London W13
Tel: 0181 567 1914/9661

Somali Action Centre
Kings Hall
Southall
0BI 1RB
Tel: 0181 606 9825

Somali Community Association
14 Featherhouse Road
Southall UB2 4RG
Tel: 0181 571 9422

Somali Self-help and Welfare Association
Uxbridge Road
London W13 8RA
Tel: 0181 205 3007

Somali Welfare Association
Oak Tree Community Centre
Osbourne Road
Acton
London W13 8TY
Tel: 0181 993 8315

Somali Women's Refugee Centre
Priory Community Centre
Acton Lane
London W13 8NY
Tel: 0181 752 1787

ENFIELD
Somali Enfield Community and Cultural Association
Wheatsheaf Hall
Main Avenue
Bush Hill Park
Enfield EN1 1DS
Tel: 0181 367 6157

GREENWICH
Somali Refugee Action Group
Clock House Community Centre
Woolwich Dockyard
London SE18 6QL
Tel: 0181 317 3447

HACKNEY
International Somali Community Trust
85E Upper Clapton Road
London E5 9BU
Tel: 0181 806 8757

HAMMERSMITH and FULHAM
Horn of Africa Community Group
St Pauls Court
Hammersmith and London College
Giddon Road
London W14 9BI
Tel: 0181 563 9145

HARINGEY
Haringey Somali Community and Cultural Association
Selby Centre
Selby Road
Tottenham
London N17 8JN
Tel: 0181 885 1307

Haringey Refugee Consortium
Selby Centre
Selby Road
Tottenham
London N17 8JN
Tel: 0181 885 5511

HARROW
Harrow Somali Refugee Consortium
27 Northhalt Road
South Harrow
HA2 0LH
Tel: 0181 864 9687

HOUNSLOW
West London Somali Association,
12 School Road
Hounslow
TW3 1QZ
Tel: 0181 577 3226

Horn of Africa Women's Asociation
13 Ruskin Road
Isleworth
TW7 6HT
Tel: 0181 560 7867

ISLINGTON
Islington Somali Community
25 Halliford Street
London N1 3HF
Tel: 0181 354 9895

KENSINGTON AND CHELSEA
Somali Welfare Assocaition
St. Jude's Crypt
25 Collingham Road
London SW5 0LX
Tel: 0171 373 3537

LAMBETH
Lambeth Somali Community Association
13/15 Stockwell Road
London SW9 9AU
Tel: 0171 738 6372

Puntland Society
365 Brixton Road
London SW9 7DP
Tel: 0171 737 0985

NEWHAM
Newham Somali Association
Froud Green Parish Office
Romford Road
London E12 5JF
Tel: 0181 470 6484

Somali Barawanese Welfare Association
28 Windsor Road
Ilford
Essex 1GL 1HQ
Tel: 0171 553 4498

SOUTHWARK
British-Somali Southwark Refugee Coucil
24 Hayward House
Benhill Road
London SE5 7NA
Tel: 0171 277 1770

Somali Counselling Project,
5 Westminister Bridge Road,
London SE1 7XW
Tel: 0171 620 4589

TOWER HAMLETS
London Black Women's Health Action Project
The Community Centre
1 Cornwall Avenue
London E2 0HW
Tel: 0181 980 3503

Somali Education and Employment Project
Island House
Church and Community Centre
London E14 3PG
Tel: 0171 480 6095

Oxford House Somali Projects
Oxford House
Derbyshire Street
London E2 6HG
Tel: 0171 739 9001

WALTHAM FOREST
Waltham Forest Somali Women's Association
William Morris Community Centre,
Greenleaf Road
Tel: 0181 521 5021

Somali Banadir Welfare Association
19 Grove Green Road
Leytonstone
London E11 5SL
Tel: 0181 521 8401